The Gospel UNCENSORED

How only grace leads to freedom

Ken Blue • Alden Swan

Cover design by: Elliot Swan

WestBow Press books may be ordered through booksellers or by contacting:

WestBow Press
A Division of Thomas Nelson
1663 Liberty Drive
Bloomington, IN 47403
www.westbowpress.com
1-(866) 928-1240

ISBN: 978-1-4497-0454-4 (sc)
ISBN: 978-1-4497-0455-1 (hc)
ISBN: 978-1-4497-0453-7 (e)

Library of Congress Control Number: 2010935749

Printed in the United States of America

WestBow Press rev. date: 10/5/2010

For Jo. Without your encouragement, this book would never have been completed.

Contents

Chapter 5: The True Source of Authority. 57

True Biblical authority derives from the truth, not from any office, position, or gift. Anyone teaching a different gospel has no authority, no matter what their position. Paul did not write to the leaders of the Galatian church, but to the congregation; it is the people of the church who hold the real authority. By Paul's own example as well as the example of Jesus, we see that true leadership is not based on power, but vulnerability.

Chapter 6: Paul's Gospel–The One True Gospel? 79

Paul was convinced that he had preached the only true Gospel, and he provided the Galatians with three pieces of evidence to support this claim: 1) Jesus personally revealed the Gospel to Paul on the road to Damascus; 2) The Apostles confirmed that Paul had the true Gospel; 3) Paul confronted and convinced Peter that he had indeed lost the Gospel by falling back into Jewish dietary laws.

Chapter 7: Peter and Paul–Confrontation and Reasons Why. . . 89

The Gospel required that Paul confront Peter because any fall into legalism has dire consequences. We know from the Bible that Peter had acted out of fear; it is also possible that Peter didn't grasp the implications of his actions. Through this encounter we see that grace must be central to everything we do.

Chapter 8: The Heart of the Gospel—Justification by Grace . . 105

Justification by grace is the foundation of all other Christian doctrines. Only the guilty can be justified; the Law declares that we are sinners, unable to justify ourselves. However, we have not only been forgiven, we have been declared righteous.

Chapter 9: Justification Continued 119

Because we have been justified, we have no fear of God's wrath. We have been made holy, and are free from the Law. The Law had no ability to justify us; this was not its purpose. The Law can show us what holy looks like, but it cannot make us holy.

Chapter 10: The Key to the Christian Life 129

The Christian life begins in grace, continues by grace, and is concluded by grace. It is folly to think that we begin life in grace, but continue on through human effort. Grace is best defined as "God's empowering presence;" the process of sanctification, of becoming Christ-like, depends upon on the Holy Spirit to produce fruit in us.

Chapter 11: The Place and Purpose of the Law............. 141

We cannot be justified by keeping the Law, nor can we be made holy through keeping the Law. Paul explains two of the purposes of the Law: First, the Law revealed our sin. Second, the Law functioned as a tutor, revealing God's holiness, but also setting a standard that no one but Jesus could attain. Thus, the Law showed us our need for a savior. Now that Jesus has come, we are no longer in need of such a tutor.

Chapter 12: Life in Christ 151

We have been set free from sin and the constraints of the Law to live a life of freedom in the Spirit. Three aspects of this new life are: 1) we have been made sons and daughters of God; 2) we are now related to every other Christian as equals; and 3) we are now descendants of Abraham, and heirs of the Covenant.

Chapter 13: What it Means to be Free.................... 163

We have been set free to live lives of freedom; however, this does not mean that we are free to sin, for sin is by nature bondage. We also have not been set free to live under legalism; the devil doesn't care what we are in bondage to, as long as we're in bondage! True freedom is freedom to live our lives serving one another in love.

Chapter 14: Understanding Internal Conflict............. 175

We often feel like we are a walking civil war, struggling with who we ought to be and who we act like we are, between the spirit and the flesh. The reality of our Christian life is that our experience doesn't always line up with what we know to be true, that we are being formed into the image of Christ. This is precisely what grace is for: Grace fills the gap between who we were in the flesh and who we are in Christ.

Chapter 15: The Reciprocal Nature of the Church 187

The church consists of reciprocal, horizontal relationships, where we all give to and receive from each other. While we have different roles and responsibilities, we are equals, and we are called to carry one another's burdens. No member of the church is above correction. Paul indicates that those who teach are giving, and in return, those who are taught should share "all good things" with their teachers. Contrary to much popular teaching, this verse does not support a rule of tithing; giving is based on grace and the reciprocal nature of church relationships.

Chapter 16: What Goes Around Comes Around, or You Reap What You Sow 201

The doctrine of grace is not opposed to the instruction to do good works; the issue is not whether we should do good works, but in what context we should do them. Sowing seeds of legalism or sin—both human efforts—produce human results.

Chapter 17: Back to the Beginning 207

As Martin Luther once said, we are always in danger of losing the Gospel. Therefore there is a need to constantly re-evangelize each other. We have been set free so that we can be formed into a new creation, through grace. It is for freedom that Christ has set us free.

Thanks... 209

CHAPTER 0: THE BEGINNING

In the summer of 1991, Ken Blue delivered a series of twelve sermons on Galatians that is the essence of this book. My wife and I had recently started attending Ken's church, having just moved to San Diego from Orange County that March. Our move was well-timed; Ken's teaching on grace was exactly what we needed to hear.

I had been raised Lutheran and was well-versed in grace; however, in my twenties I began to encounter Christians who had been raised to see Christianity in terms of dos and don'ts and who insisted there were things I had to do in order to become a "better" Christian. I saw the agony that people went through trying to follow rules, and the feelings of guilt they suffered because they were never quite good enough. Some tired of the agony and simply gave up.

A few years after my wife and I moved to Southern California, we were exposed to several Bible teachers who had some good things to say but whose teaching on holiness and works as a requirement for God's blessings contradicted my understanding of grace. This constant tension between grace and legalism bothered me, and I decided it was time to study the issue until I finally understood it. It was at this point that we first heard Ken Blue speak.

Ken's no-nonsense teaching of Paul's no-nonsense letter to the Galatians clarified the issues of the Law and the Gospel for me like nothing else had. Over the years I listened to the series several times, discovering that I never tired of hearing Paul's radical Good News preached.

I still love to hear the real Gospel preached. I believe that we *need* to hear and be reminded of the Good News. We are being bombarded from all sides with bad news. At the office we hear that we must "do more and try harder." The people on TV and radio tell us that we're not happy enough or sexy enough without whatever it is they are selling. Nowhere else do we hear that we are completely accepted and valued regardless of our performance. The Gospel is more than just "how to get saved," preparing us for life after death. It really is the good news for our lives *before* death. This Good News—the truth—will indeed set us free, here and now.

Very early on I began to conceive of Ken's sermon series as a book, initially as a mildly edited version of the sermons, and began to work off transcriptions of the sermon tapes. However, I kept thinking of things that *I'd* like to say, and finally I decided to write a completely new book around the sermon material, adding my own thoughts and ideas along the way. The result could perhaps be thought of as "Variations on a theme by Ken Blue." Thankfully, Ken's response to an early draft of the book was, "It is better than the original."

Collaborative works, as this became, can sometimes be rather clumsy trying to balance the thoughts of two authors. As I have followed the general outline of Ken's *Freedom in Christ* sermon series, I elected to write consistently in Ken's voice (aside from this prologue and a short epilogue). I have, therefore, used "I" rather than the shifting to the occasional "we," taking the risk of sometimes putting words in Ken's mouth. I have, however, attempted to identify who is speaking where it seemed necessary to do so.

While Ken and I come from different backgrounds and will disagree on various points of theology, we agree on the centrality of the Gospel to the whole of the Christian life and we are both passionate about this message. It causes me pain—and admittedly a fair amount of anger—to see people buried under religious burdens that they were never meant to carry. Some of the perpetrators of legalism are simply ignorant and possibly suffering under religious burdens themselves. Others are not so innocent, using religion as a means to control others. I have sympathy for the former, but not for the latter. Those who know me well can tell you that I have no tolerance whatsoever for legalism; whatever the motivation, the consequences are the same: abused, confused and damaged people, and a loss of the Gospel.

While this book contains a bit of theology, *The Gospel Uncensored* is primarily the retelling of stories. The main story is of a missionary writing to a young church that had been led astray and needed to better understand the Gospel. Within that story there are other stories: We read about a leader who failed but was set back on course, about the giving of laws to a very rebellious people, and about a promise God made to a man and his children. As we look at these stories, we discover that they are also stories about us, because things haven't changed that much—at any point we can find ourselves in stories just like these. Paul's words, we discover, are as pertinent today as they were in the first century.

It is my sincere hope that this book will bring freedom and peace to those who have struggled with legalism, that faith will be restored where it has been lost and new faith found where none existed.

Above all, be free. For it is truly for freedom that Christ has set us free.

Alden Swan

May, 2010

CHAPTER 1: LOSING MY RELIGION

Ken's Story

Like many of you, I had a very dramatic conversion; by the time I was saved, I was an experienced, accomplished sinner. When Jesus saved me, I had every vice and bad habit imaginable. Yet, I found myself fully accepted by Him and through that encounter, I was radically changed. Not that I was perfected at that moment—even years later, I have a long way to go—but something began to happen at that moment to make me an entirely different person. I could and still can say with Paul, "All things have become a new." Not all things have become perfect, but we have a whole new ball game, so to speak.

The chronic sense of failure, futility, and meaninglessness that had hung like a shadow over my life disappeared in an instant. I suddenly saw that I could be a part God's mission to this world and started to tell other people about the Jesus who found me, accepted me the way I was, and who now carried my load for me. Many of them grabbed hold of the Gospel, and I saw them converted and their lives changed.

This was in 1967, during the Vietnam War, soon after I had been drafted. Because I was in the army, the first two years of my

Christian life were completely outside the sphere of any organized Christian group or church. I did meet the occasional Christian and I exchanged letters with some Christian friends I made, but I was essentially unchurched. I didn't attend church every Sunday, nor did I have any contact with a regular community of believers.

The Natural Christian Life

Because there were no Christians around to disciple me, or even explain what had happened to me, I didn't fully understand the power of God's grace. I had no idea what kind of radical, new life had been vectored into me. Very mysteriously the Holy Spirit began to work in me and I was able to observe its effects on my life. I found that I automatically and naturally began to delight in some things that I used to hate, and in the same way I began hating—without anyone exhorting or prompting me—the things that I had once loved.

Many of my big, nasty sins suddenly left me, as if they were no big deal. It's not that I didn't continue to struggle with sin, but many of them simply stopped being issues for me. No one told me that Christians should not do this or that; I had been born again and was a changed man. It all happened automatically and I thought, *This is the Christian life? How in the world did they keep this a secret from me for all these years?*

As you can imagine, I still didn't have a clue what the Christian life was really about. I can remember feeling somewhat sheepish that I read the New Testament for the first time at the age of twenty-one. As I read Matthew, I thought, *Well, that's interesting, that's who Jesus is; I wonder what Mark's about?* I looked at Mark, and to my surprise it was the same story! Then I looked at Luke, and thought, *My gosh, these are all the same story!* I was twenty-one years old, had lived my whole life in America, and was completely unaware that Matthew,

Mark, Luke and John were actually different versions of the same story! It came as a complete surprise to me. That's how clueless I was about Christianity.

Although I was without any kind of Christian community for those first two years, I actually had a fairly sound Christian education. This is even more remarkable considering that I had attended college for two years, but was still a functional illiterate. Honestly, I couldn't read. But that hadn't mattered, as I was one of those who got by on an athletic scholarship. However, one of the side effects of my conversion was that I started reading! The first book I ever read—not just the first Christian book, mind you, but the first book in my entire life—was *Mere Christianity* by C. S. Lewis. I then read everything from Lewis that I could get my hands on. So, my Christian education for the first two years consisted of the Bible, C. S. Lewis, and A. W. Tozer—and, of course, the Holy Spirit at work in me.

Another interesting effect of my conversion was that without being taught, I prayed, a lot. I started talking to God and carrying on a conversation with Him on a more or less constant basis. I even *sang* prayers; nobody told me to do that. I would go off where no one could hear me, and I would sing prayers to God because it seemed the only natural way to express what was inside of me. In other words, I knew instinctively how to worship before I was ever in a worship service or had worship modeled for me.

After the army I returned to college, and for the first time in my life, I was an excellent student. I had been a dumb jock before I was converted, but now suddenly I was a scholar. I took my faith very seriously, and made up my mind that I was going to knuckle down and be the best Christian that I could be. This determination to excel at being a Christian soon proved to be a mixed blessing.

This stage of my Christian life became extremely full. In addition to carrying a full load at school, being on two athletic teams, holding down a part-time job, and helping to take care of my grandmother, I taught Sunday School at a Presbyterian church and studied the Bible at a fundamentalist seminary. I also became involved in InterVarsity Christian Fellowship on campus. It never occurred to me that there were any theological differences in these groups; I just assumed it was all one and the same.

Death by Church

I was now well into the Christian world and for the first time I began to relate with and learn from the church and church-related groups. And, over that first year, the spontaneous life that had been given to me so freely began to die.

Like many of you, I started the Christian life full of joy, full of optimism, full of excitement. And, perhaps like many of you, after two years the joy was already gone. Looking back now, it is quite obvious how it happened: The things that I used to do naturally out of joy, out of sheer gratitude, or because it was simply the Holy Spirit leading me, I was now being told that I *had* to do in order to maintain fellowship with God. What had been *expressions* of my life in Christ were now *expectations* of my life in Christ.

I thought that if I jumped through these religious hoops—if I performed well enough—God would give me a passing grade and I could continue having fellowship with Him and excel at being a Christian. Instead of good works done out of joy, these became *my* end of the contract. When I started thinking that God *required* me to do things in order for me to gain His approval, I started hating them.

However, *I still did them!* I thought that this was simply what Christians do—they do stuff that they hate in order to please God.

In a few short months I had fallen into a pattern of seeing the Christian life as a burdensome crown of thorns, presenting my body as a "dying sacrifice," instead of seeing it as the spontaneous life in Christ.

This "do more, try harder" kind of life went on for many years. Because I was not the kind of person to do anything half way, I did everything all the way. I became a pastor and worked hard to become the best pastor that I could be. However, fifteen years into my Christian life, I was done. My marriage was a mess, I had bleeding ulcers, I had chronic pain throughout my body, I was depressed, and I was mentally and emotionally unstable. I said to God, "I'm only 35 years old. I'm done! If this is it, I'm the wrong person for this job. So either you get me another job, or show me how to do this one right."

Grace Revisited

At some point—I don't remember why, maybe I thought if I tried hard enough I could figure it out and put the pieces together—I began to take another look at the New Testament. What I found was that life comes as a gift, and not as something that we earn! Fascinated with this thing called grace, I began working through it systematically, and then I began preaching it. Wonder of wonders, I saw that it worked—everybody else was getting free from legalism! Sooner or later, I thought, it was going to work for me.

I studied and taught grace for several years before I could see results in my own life, but slowly it began to take hold in me. I finally started to seriously believe that the whole Christian life, not just your initial salvation, is free. I started believing that it is all about God's love and acceptance, and that all of His gifts and ministry are free to me simply because this is the way God wants it, and not for any other reason! My own efforts were of no benefit.

Believing, thinking, preaching this truth, and convincing other people that the Gospel really is "Jesus plus nothing" gradually had an impact; truth began to seep into me. Now, many years later, I can say that I'm almost recovered. I'm still angry, as you can probably tell, but I've almost gotten over it. Now, the greatest joy that I have is being able to help other people out of the same trap that I fell into, and preventing new converts from ever falling into the trap in the first place.

This is why I love Paul's letter to the Galatians. The book of Galatians is so helpful to the Church because it explains to us how the fire dies, and it helps us release the fire again. To further illustrate this point, let me tell you one more story.

One More Story

Several years ago I was in Canada doing some conferences that dealt mainly with healing spiritual abuse. After one of the sessions a woman came up to me with two friends. This is the basic story that she told me: At fourteen years old she was a prostitute on the streets. She was used and abused, full of shame, pain, and self-hatred. Then, in one of those very dramatic encounters, Jesus saves her and she is transformed overnight. Without anybody making her, she stops her line of work. She gets plugged into straight society. She gets a job at a warehouse doing something clerical, and she's off to the races.

Because she knew that Jesus was not ashamed of her, she didn't have any problems telling everyone in the world about Jesus. She had a special ability, a gift, to walk up to people, totally disarm them, get right in their face and tell them about Jesus. You can imagine that a woman who's been a prostitute since the age of fourteen is not afraid of anything. One after another, she'd lead people to Christ, get them plugged into a church, and then she'd go out and talk to somebody else. Evangelism was as natural for her as going out for pizza. She was full of God's grace, power and love.

At some point, however, the fire started to die. She had heard some bad teaching about how she had to be good enough for God to use her, and good enough to make it through the end times. Because she was such an open, trusting person, when this so-called Christian authority figure comes along and tells her "you don't qualify, yet" she believed it.

She became depressed, her self-hatred returned, and the joy that she once possessed had left. She said through tears, "I'm so ashamed of what I've become. I used to be able to talk to people, and I used to be able have communion with God. I don't anymore. I feel bad, and the worse thing is *I'm afraid to tell anyone about Jesus for fear that they'll say yes and end up as miserable as me.*"

I exposed the lie that she had been fed and once again preached to her the Good News of the Gospel. We prayed for a while, and eventually she breathed deeply and leaned back against the wall. She reached out and put her arms around her friends on each side of her and said, "OK, let's go to the mall, I'm back."

This is what returning to God's grace will do for you! Your life is underneath there, smoldering, and if you'd only let God's grace take hold of you, it'll come back. It will fire back into flames, and more of what you have been giving will be given back to you, in more ways than you can imagine.

Dear Galatians, Love Paul

Paul's letter to the Galatians is so helpful to us because of the very reason that Paul wrote it. Paul didn't just wake up some morning and think, "I feel sort of theological this morning. I think I'll write something about Jesus to some people. Let's see, let's send this off to the Corinthians, and this off to the Ephesians." No, these are what are called *ad hoc* ("for this purpose") documents; he was responding to a specific problem in a specific church, and his letter to the Galatians was to correct a specific issue.

Paul had planted the church in Galatia, and it had been founded on Paul's Gospel of grace. Paul's message was that Christ *is* forgiveness for sin; Christ *is* our relationship with God; Christ *is* life after death. Christ is, more importantly, life *before* death. Paul's message was "It's all yours simply for the believing."

Then, after Paul had appointed elders and left Galatia, some people came and began teaching that belief in Jesus was not enough. These likely were some converted Jews from Jerusalem who had received Jesus as Lord and Savior, but who felt that they had to hang on to the law and Judaism. Four thousand years of Jewish traditions were hard for some to give up. They thought that Christianity ought to be an updated version of Judaism and couldn't accept that Gentiles could be included into the Church, much less allowed to remain as Gentiles.

These teachers came to the Galatians and said something like, "Listen, we're here to follow up and improve on Paul's ministry to you. He was absolutely right in saying that you need to have faith in Jesus—that's how you get started in the Christian life. What he failed to tell you, and what he would have told you if he had time, is that in addition to Jesus you need to follow certain religious laws and rules."

This is exactly what happened to me, what may have happened to you, and what has happened to countless people who have been Christians for any length of time. Your relationship with God was initially free. It filled you with joy. Your first experience with the Holy Spirit was intoxicating and wonderful. You thought, *This is it!* Then someone almost immediately said, "If you want to become a *good* Christian, you need to have your quiet time, tithe, evangelize, and so on. We're just looking after your best interests. Yes, of course Jesus, but Jesus plus these other good things—this is the Christian life. Paul is right so far as he goes, but he didn't go far enough, and we're to take you on to maturity."

Jesus Plus Nothing

The religious formula these teachers were using was—and this is a phrase that I will use over and over again—"Jesus plus something." Paul was livid about this because he knew and was convinced that the true equation is *Jesus plus nothing equals salvation.* He also recognized that any time someone teaches "Jesus plus something," even if it is just a little something, they are not improving on the Gospel, or even distracting from the Gospel. Teaching Jesus plus something *is the utter destruction of the Gospel.*

Getting over "Jesus plus religion" is what Paul's letter to the Galatians is about. Getting over "Jesus plus something" is what will allow freedom and the fire to come back. It will allow the Spirit to produce life in us, and in the Church.

My assumption is that you do not need a higher revelation. People say, "You know, my spiritual life is a little dull. I need a higher revelation. I need a conference. I want to hear something new or something this or something that." I think conferences are good; we put on conferences for a lot of good reasons, and I speak at many of them. But the reason is not so that you can get a higher revelation or hear something that somebody has never heard before. You just need to rehear the Gospel, and believe what you believed the first time, because that is the truth.

Jesus plus nothing is your salvation and your life. You don't need to hear something new. However, you may need to delete some of the stuff that you were taught on top of the Gospel. You don't need another conference where you can go forward and recommit your life yet one more time, to try to get it right *this* time, or *really* repent of sin. You don't need that. What you need is to *sense* the life of God that was always in you and never left you. You need to have confidence that Christianity is not you hanging on to Jesus, which comes down to your performance, but that it is Jesus hanging on to you. It's His life in you that is the Christian walk.

I believe the power of the Word of God will do everything in you that needs to be done. I often get criticized for not demanding more of people in terms of spiritual discipline. But you see, this is not my idea; I just believe the Bible.

My confidence is not in my ability to badger anyone into straightening up. What I do have is confidence in God's Spirit that is in us and in the Word that I preach. I believe that this word will do its work. I believe that all we have to do is preach the Gospel and the light and the life that has dimmed or has been lost will come back. The Word will produce life. My theory is that if I can put people in touch with the Light of the World, the Light will take care of the rest. Fire will burn, life will live, and grace will change lives.

If you put your faith in Jesus as opposed to faith in doing this thing or that thing, what you are going to discover is that your Christian life, like a good marriage, gets better with time. It doesn't cool off, it heats up. Some of you think, "Boy, it would be great to be in that first flush of love with Jesus." However, in truth it wouldn't, because there's something coming that is even better than the honeymoon stage of our Christianity. Do you really think that the normal Christian life is meant to begin in tremendous excitement and joy, but that as you get to know God more you find that you don't like him as much and you aren't as excited about him? Do you understand how totally crazy that is?

Knowing Jesus, experiencing Jesus and loving Jesus gets better with time. You get hotter. You get stronger. The relationship gets more passionate, more intense. That's what you have to look forward to. I'll tell you from personal experience, I wouldn't give you anything for the first few years of my marriage compared with the last few years. Our marriage is better now than it ever was. I have to believe that according to the curve, it's going to get even better. That's how real relationships with interesting people like my wife work. And that's how a relationship with Jesus works.

To me, the key verse in Galatians is 5:1, "It is for freedom that Christ has set us free." The Gospel that Paul contends for in his letter to the Galatians is quite simple, a frustrating thing to those inclined to rules and regulations or who wish to use religion to control people. It was this same Gospel truth for which Martin Luther and the other reformers contended—and were persecuted for—many years ago, and for which I contend today.

"Jesus plus nothing" (*solus Christus* to the reformers) is our foundation. To add anything at all to the work of Jesus in either saving or perfecting us is to create a counterfeit gospel, one which is "no gospel at all" (Gal. 1:7), and which brings death instead of life. To further affirm that we can add nothing to what Christ has done, the reformers identified two other foundational beliefs, *sola gratia* and *sola fide*: by grace alone, and by faith alone. As Paul wrote in Ephesians 2:8-9, "For it is by grace you have been saved, through faith—and this not from yourselves, it is the gift of God— not by works, so that no one can boast." This is how we are saved, and this is the way we are to live, for "it is for freedom that Christ has set us free."

Losing The Gospel

We are in danger of losing the Gospel. In fact, in many churches—including those we think of as very evangelical churches—it has already been lost. I do not mean merely misplaced or muddled; I mean it has been tossed out the window in favor of fraudulent, interloping gospels that are in reality no Gospel at all. I do not mean to suggest that this is a recent state of affairs, or that it is even surprising; the Gospel message has been under attack from the very beginning. Within twenty-five or thirty years of Jesus' death and resurrection, the Gospel had already been lost in Galatia, a region which had been evangelized by Paul. In response, Paul wrote a letter that has helped protect the Gospel for two thousand years—the book of Galatians—a letter as applicable today as it was in AD 58.

Nearly five hundred years ago, a Roman Catholic priest named Martin Luther discovered the Gospel had once again been lost, and within a few short years after the Reformation began, he saw signs that the Gospel was once again in danger from new forms of legalism. His response? To once again teach through the book of Galatians. In the introduction to his *Commentary on the Epistle to the Galatians*, Luther wrote,

> I have taken in hand, in the name of the Lord, once again to expound the Epistle of St. Paul to the Galatians; not because I desire to teach new things, or such as you have not heard before, but because we have to fear, as the greatest and nearest danger, that Satan take from us the pure doctrine of faith and bring into the Church again the doctrine of works and men's traditions.
>
> The devil, our adversary, who continually seeks to devour us, is not dead; likewise our flesh and old man is yet alive. Besides this, all kinds of temptations vex and oppress us on every side. So this doctrine can never be taught, urged, and repeated enough. If this doctrine is lost, then is also the whole knowledge of the truth, life and salvation lost. If this doctrine flourishes, then all good things flourish.

Luther's comments are no less applicable today. The greatest danger to Christianity today comes not from humanism, atheism, or materialism, but from a far more insidious source: the legalism that exists in the church. Legalism slips in when we least expect it, and it's often hard to recognize. Most Christians understand that we are saved by grace through faith in Christ. To suggest that we need to do something to earn our way "in" is unthinkable. This is, after all, what the Reformation was all about. But what about life after we are saved? What *does* God expect of us?

In thinking about possible answers to this question, I did a fair amount of googling on the topic. It was very interesting to see that many pastors and laypeople took a strong stand against what they saw as legalism but yet failed to recognize their own legalism. Some did recognize this apparent incongruity in their teachings and went to great lengths to explain why the other laws were bad and their own were good. Legalists typically don't see themselves as legalists; if anything, they are "obedient." They may judge negatively the church across the street for their rules against dancing (man's law), but preach that Christians are required to tithe (God's law). What is the difference? In truth, there is none; you either believe you can earn something from God or you don't. Your choice is legalism or grace—there is no middle ground.

Legalism is the belief that you can or must add any human effort to the work of Christ, either with regard to salvation (justification) or holiness (sanctification). The Gospel is not merely about getting "saved." The good news is, as Paul writes in Galatians 5:1, "It is for freedom that Christ has set us free." Grace is certainly our starting point, but it is also how we finish. As John Newton penned in *Amazing Grace*,

> 'Tis Grace that brought me safe thus far and Grace will
> lead me home.

If we turn to our own efforts—works—at any point, we not only miss out on grace, we completely annihilate the Gospel. This is precisely what Paul's letter to the Galatians is about. Paul saw this issue as of the utmost importance in the first century; as such, the letter to the Galatians stands out among Paul's epistles due to its urgent—and angry—tone. Likewise, Luther was not exaggerating in the least when he wrote, "If this doctrine is lost, then is also the whole knowledge of the truth, life and salvation lost." Nor am I exaggerating when I say it is no less crucial today that we continue to contend for the Gospel. This is why I have dedicated my life to the plain and simple message of the radical Gospel of grace, and the reason for this book. The message in the book of Galatians can never be repeated enough.

CHAPTER 2: THE TROUBLE WITH THE GALATIANS

A person doesn't have to read far into Paul's letter to the Galatians to see that he was quite upset when he wrote it. The Galatians had allowed some teachers from outside of Galatia (presumably, as I have mentioned, some Christians of Jewish descent) to convince them to abandon true life in Christ for that lived under the Law. Paul could not believe that anyone would want to do such a thing, and it obviously infuriated him. He begins his letter as follows:

> Paul, an apostle—sent not from men nor by man, but by Jesus Christ and God the Father, who raised him from the dead— and all the brothers with me, To the churches in Galatia:
>
> Grace and peace to you from God our Father and the Lord Jesus Christ, who gave himself for our sins to rescue us from the present evil age, according to the will of our God and Father, to whom be glory for ever and ever. Amen.
>
> I am astonished that you are so quickly deserting the one who called you by the grace of Christ and are turning

> to a different gospel—which is really no gospel at all. Evidently some people are throwing you into confusion and are trying to pervert the gospel of Christ. But even if we or an angel from heaven should preach a gospel other than the one we preached to you, let him be eternally condemned! As we have already said, so now I say again: If anybody is preaching to you a gospel other than what you accepted, let him be eternally condemned!
>
> Am I now trying to win the approval of men, or of God? Or am I trying to please men? If I were still trying to please men, I would not be a servant of Christ. (Galatians 1:1-10)

Notice that when Paul writes to this particular church, he quickly follows up his introduction and blessing with a stinging, sharp rebuke. He says (my paraphrase), "I am astonished, I am amazed, and I am absolutely dumbfounded that you are so quickly deserting the one who called you by His grace, and turning instead in utter disloyalty to another gospel, which really is no gospel at all. Have I wasted my time with you?"

If you skim through the rest of Paul's letters you will see that Paul is doing something completely uncharacteristic here. In the opening chapters of Romans, Colossians or Paul's other letters, he says, "I never stop giving thanks for you," or things of that nature. Yet to the Galatians he includes no such pleasantries; he writes, in fact, in an entirely different tone. Take a look at Paul's introduction in First Corinthians:

> I always thank God for you because of his grace given you in Christ Jesus. For in him you have been enriched in every way—in all your speaking and in all your knowledge— because our testimony about Christ was

> confirmed in you. Therefore you do not lack any spiritual gift as you eagerly wait for our Lord Jesus Christ to be revealed. He will keep you strong to the end, so that you will be blameless on the day of our Lord Jesus Christ. God, who has called you into fellowship with his Son Jesus Christ our Lord, is faithful. (1 Cor. 1:4-9)

Remember to whom Paul is writing, and the issues he is dealing with here. This is, after all, another *ad hoc* letter—that is, it was written with a purpose. Remember the unbelievably immoral lives these people were living, the spiritual and physical hanky-panky, getting drunk at communion services, sleeping with step-mothers, and everything else? Paul wrote this as a letter of correction, yet he says, "I am so grateful for you. Your testimony is being heard everywhere. I haven't wasted my time with you."

Who would think that this is how he would greet the Corinthians? I would have expected him to say to the Corinthians, "Come on, you guys. You're hanging out with temple prostitutes. Don't you know any better? Have I wasted my time with you?" Isn't that what you or I would say? Instead, Paul saves this kind of language for the straight-laced, religious, conservative Christian people of Galatia:

> Are you observing special days or months, trying to be religious, trying to be good, trying to please man by your religious disciplines? I fear for you that somehow that I've wasted my efforts on you. (Gal. 4:10,11 my paraphrase)

The Galatians were people who were desperately trying to be good—working on all the Christians disciplines—and these are the people about whom he wonders if he's wasted his time.

His values are so opposite from ours that it's absolutely shocking. But, as it turns out, they are right in line with those of

Jesus. Remember that Jesus was known as the friend of sinners. He fellowshipped with prostitutes and tax collectors, and he hung out with criminals. He called them God's people and told them they were close to the kingdom of God. However, he called the Pharisees and teachers—who paid their tithes, memorized the Bible, and kept all of the laws—"whitewashed tombs" and snakes. (Matt. 23:23,27)

Jesus didn't say, "Beware the yeast of the prostitutes, tax collectors, and pimps." Rather, he said, "Beware of the yeast of the Pharisees" (Matt. 16). Those are Jesus' values as recorded in the Gospels, and those are Paul's values in this letter. Paul is angry about people adding works to the Gospel. However, he doesn't have the same kind of problem with some of the Corinthians who are acting like a bunch of wild animals; they, at least, haven't lost the Gospel. Paul chastises the Corinthians but we see that Paul treats behavioral issues differently than Gospel issues. For Paul, sin is an issue, but it's secondary; the Gospel is always primary.

The Lost Gospel

To understand Paul's statements here, we must realize that the Galatians had indeed lost the Gospel—not just watered it down or confused it a bit, but actually lost it—because somebody added something to the simple "saved by grace through faith in Jesus" message. They had added religious disciplines as a requirement for being in relationship with God. To this Paul says, "That doesn't merely mess things up a little bit; that entirely wipes it out. I've wasted my time. I've utterly wasted my time with you."

Paul obviously didn't believe the Galatians were a lost cause, for the mere fact that he wrote this letter. However, we need to look at the point that Paul made here: In the event that he could not correct this error, the Galatians were, indeed, a lost cause—a waste of his time. But, what would make them a lost cause? A good percentage of the church today has compromised the Gospel in similar ways, and very few people get this upset; was Paul perhaps overreacting? Assuming that Paul was not overreacting and this issue is as important as Paul seems to think it is, we should try to understand what the issue is for Paul.

Another way to look at the question is this: Why are those who struggle with sin—those who keep looking to Jesus for forgiveness and relationship rather than in religious works—closer to the Kingdom of God than those who seemingly have their act together and are proud of it? The reason is, perhaps, that sinners know they are *not* good enough, and *can't* be good enough, so they are relying on Jesus to save them. They are not tempted to have faith in their own works, and are by necessity looking to God for mercy. The religious folks, on the other hand—the circumcised Christians, in the context of Galatians—look to themselves and begin relying on their own power and good works.

I am not against the spiritual disciplines, by the way (and for that matter, have nothing against circumcision); in fact, I encourage you to read the Bible, have quiet times, tithe regularly (more on this in Chapter 15), stop sinning, and do many, many good works. However, don't think for one minute that they will give you any more favor, power, or spiritual brownie points with God; everything that God gives is free! When you miss this point, it's not that you're just a little bit off target; you've missed *everything* about the Gospel.

When you look at yourself and your performance, and you try to do better or jump through hoops hoping that it will somehow be pleasing to God, you forget that God has already said that human attempts at righteousness are not good enough. Yes, repent of your sins, but *repent of the things you do right, too*, because they still fall short of perfection. Jesus is the only man who ever did anything that pleased God in terms of performance. For this reason, you had better believe in Jesus and trust in his performance on your behalf, or you are one dead duck.

Live Free—Or Die

The Gospel is all or nothing—you either trust God to love you because of Jesus' performance and put absolutely no confidence in your own works, or you are dead; the Gospel is null and void for you. But, if you're struggling, if you're sinning, but you are still depending on God, then you are on the right (the narrow) road.

This is how it works: You know that you are a wretched sinner and you know that you have fallen short. You say, "God, help me. If you don't correct me, I'm always going to be this way, but I am depending on you." That is the way you stay connected to the vine (John 15:5). But when you turn from Him, and say "Okay, God, thanks for forgiving me; now I think I can really do this," you have just turned away from God, and rejected the Gospel. You've cut yourself off from the vine.

Since most of us are more acquainted with electricity than with vines, let me update the analogy: What happens when you take an appliance plug out of a socket? The current breaks. Life stops. The appliance has been cut off from the source. This is what adding anything to Jesus does to you. You can't "plug in" to more than one socket—if you want to plug into good works as your source of life, you have to unplug from Jesus. Take a look at any electrical appliance, and you will notice that it is designed for only one specific kind of outlet. If it is not plugged in, it's not going to function. If you could manage to plug it in to anything else it will either fail to work or do something a bit more spectacular—perhaps giving you the shock of your life! We are all designed the same way; we either plug into Jesus, or we're dead, one way or another.

What I and many others have experienced is this: Once we were plugged in to Jesus; we were infatuated with Him. All we could think about was Jesus and what He had done for us, and the Holy Spirit's life and power were flooding in to us. Then, somebody tells us, "Okay, now to be a good Christian, you've got to stop sinning, read your Bible daily, and so on." So, wanting to be a great Christian, we begin to work hard to stop sinning and read our Bibles and do whatever else—and life stops happening. To make matters even worse, we start to think "Oh, this is just the way it's supposed to be."

What is insidious about this is that we actually begin to think that if we work harder at these things, we'll regain life. But in reality, working harder only brings death; when you work harder, you unplug from Jesus. Life is given to you. It's free. Turn back to the Gospel—plug yourself back into Jesus by simply believing that you don't have to add anything to what he's already done for you—and life (and good works) will start flowing into you once again.

A Different Gospel

Paul's assessment of the situation with the Galatians was that they had lost the Gospel—a very serious pronouncement. They weren't just "fuzzy" on a few points that had to be cleared up—no, they had turned to a different gospel, a gospel that has nothing to do with *the* Gospel. When Paul talks about a "different" gospel he uses the Greek word *heteros*, which means "different" in the same way we would say that apples are different from rocks. There should be no confusion here—there is something edible and life-giving on one hand and something entirely different and dead on the other. Paul tells the Galatians that they have chosen a different gospel—which does not have any power to save or bring life.

Paul is not talking "different" in the sense that you have a Dodge instead of a Chevy; they are both cars, and will both get you to your destination. What Paul is talking about is something that is in a different category completely, like the difference between a Dodge and a coffin. The coffin won't get you anywhere, except dead in the ground. Adding anything to Jesus—to the Gospel of grace—is not actually adding; it is subtracting. It destroys the effect of Jesus in your life altogether. Paul says, and I'll state this over and over again: Life in Christ is Jesus plus nothing.

To say "Jesus plus anything"—even to say Jesus plus something good—is to pervert and counteract the Gospel. To say that to be saved you need Jesus plus cod liver oil or something equally as revolting is just stupid; people will resist that, and hopefully find it suspicious. However, to tell people that they *must* pray, *must* read the Bible, or *must* overcome some particular sin (all good things in themselves) to be a "real" Christian is insidious; it confuses the natural work of the Spirit with human effort. It is pulling a spiritual sleight-of-hand, where the real Gospel disappears and a false one put in its place—and no one notices. In this way, the legalism that exists in many churches today is even worse than the example in Galatians.

Let's look again at verses six and seven:

> I am astonished that you are so quickly deserting the one who called you by the grace of Christ and are turning to a different gospel—which is really no gospel at all.

Not only did the Galatians desert Jesus—they didn't just mess up some teachings, they deserted Jesus himself—but they didn't wait around. This was not a long-term cooling-off process, but it seems that they couldn't wait to trade the Good News in for some religious methodology. There are various psychological, emotional, and spiritual reasons explaining why people are so quick to turn away from the truth, and we'll look at this in the next couple of chapters. However, having an explanation doesn't give the Galatians or anyone else an excuse. They had been given the clear Gospel, as have we.

For some of you, this Good News is going to come across as really bad news; like the Pharisees, you are pretty thrilled with being able to keep the rules better than the rest, and you have already been decorating your wing of the Heavenly Mansion and building display shelves for your crowns. If you want to hang on to this fantasy that you can somehow work yourself into Heaven, then there's not much anyone can do but pray for you.

However, you might be realizing that you have just wasted a good portion of your life on some religious pseudo-gospel that has not gotten you anywhere. Your Christian life may have started out well, but you've unplugged from the true Gospel that could bring you life.

Real Good News

The Good News is that whether you, like the Galatians, couldn't wait to turn away or whether you have had a more gradual cooling off period, there is hope. And, unlike the Galatians, you may *never* have known the real Gospel and are hearing it now for the first time; for you, too, there is hope. If for any reason you have bought into some false, perverse gospel, I want you to know that help is here. If you want the true life that comes from a true relationship with Jesus, you can have it. If it had been too late for the Galatians to recover grace, Paul wouldn't have written to them. The Good News is always the Good News.

Whatever has happened to you in the past is over and dead. You can't do anything about the past. So what if some preacher, organization, or teaching has robbed spontaneity from you—acknowledge it, confess it, forgive whoever needs forgiving, and let it go, because the past is dead and gone. Your real life is not in the past; your life is here and now, and in the future. You can't change the past. What you need now is to simply receive this free gift. It was free then and it is free now. You don't have to do anything to get yourself ready for grace; if that is what you are thinking, you've missed the point! There is nothing you can do but accept the free gift of grace.

CHAPTER 3: THE GOSPEL: JESUS PLUS NOTHING

The Gospel message preached by Jesus and Paul—the Good News—is more wonderful than anything any human could have invented. On the other hand, the teachings of all other religions (all human inventions) without fail involve things that *we* must do in order to achieve the promised goal. Only the true Gospel of Christianity clearly states that there is absolutely nothing you or I need to do—or for that matter *can* do—to become holy and righteous, and joint-heirs with Christ.

The simple truth of the Gospel is misunderstood by almost everybody, including many Christians. The concept of being good in order to get to Heaven is so prevalent, most people believe—or want to believe—that this is indeed the Gospel. I [Alden] was once having lunch with an attorney who claimed to have no particular religious beliefs; however, being a lawyer, he thought he had things figured out, telling me, "I just try to be the best person I can be, because I figure that no matter what religion turns out to be true, that's got to count for something." He was totally shocked when I replied that his being good was absolutely worthless! After I explained the Gospel to him, he replied, "I have never heard anything like that in my life."

The Christian Gospel is the only no-strings-attached message ever preached. Why then would anyone toss it away in favor of some imitation gospel that requires us to work for our salvation?

Paul's letter to the Galatians makes it clear that the true Gospel is not pleasing to man's sinful nature. Why is this so? What causes people to desire to try to live up to unattainable standards of fasting, prayer, and religiosity? What makes people go to churches where they get brow-beaten by legalistic preaching every Sunday? What makes people trade love, peace, and joy for guilt and shame that comes with not measuring up? This is literally what thousands of people do, and what is even worse is that there is no shortage of preachers to accommodate them.

The issue with the Galatians was not that they were merely legalistic; I think had this been the case, Paul would have written saying, "Have I got some good news for you!" No, the Galatians had already heard the true Gospel and had begun as Christians living a life of freedom, empowered by the Holy Spirit. Paul had not short-changed them on this point. The issue with the Galatians was that they had received the truth from Paul, but still were willing to exchange it all for a life of religion. Paul was astounded that anyone could make such an error.

Religion defined

I should explain that I am not using the word "religion" here in the broad sense that Christianity is one of the world religions. I am using the terms "religion" and "religious" as they are sometimes used within Christianity to refer to beliefs, practices, and behaviors which resemble those used in *other* religions; that is, works and rituals which are meant to produce spiritual gain. Going to church on Sunday because we believe we will gain points—or perhaps not *lose* points—is religious. Going to church because we long to worship

God and be with His people is not. In this sense, true Christianity is not religious—it's not about following rules, it's about knowing and relating to God.

The religious teachers who followed Paul to Galatia apparently taught that faith in Jesus is a good start for the Christian life, but to gain maturity—to enter into the deeper things of God, qualify for His highest purposes, and be a first-class, elite Christian—you need to add a religious practice, in this case, circumcision (a pretty extreme religious observance!). They didn't overtly deny Jesus, they *added something* to Jesus. In other words, their gospel became a new formula: Jesus plus circumcision equals life. However, this formula is an out-and-out lie; it doesn't add up. Jesus plus anything else equals a complete loss of the Gospel. For the visually-oriented readers, here is the Gospel formula:

Jesus = Life

Or more specifically:

Jesus + Nothing = Life

But, when you try to add anything to Jesus, this is what happens:

Jesus + Anything = – Life = Death

Again (because I can't say this enough), anytime you try to add anything whatsoever to what Jesus has already accomplished, you lose.

Those Foolish Galatians

Galatians chapter 3:1-5 is really the center of the letter:

> You foolish Galatians! Who has bewitched you? Before your very eyes Jesus Christ was clearly portrayed as crucified. I would like to learn just one thing from you:

> Did you receive the Spirit by observing the law, or by believing what you heard? Are you so foolish? After beginning with the Spirit, are you now trying to attain your goal by human effort? Have you suffered so much for nothing—if it really was for nothing? Does God give you his Spirit and work miracles among you because you observe the law, or because you believe what you heard?

He says to the Galatians, "You stupid Galatians, you began in the Spirit simply by believing; you entered into life and received the power of the Spirit, and God continues do miracles in your midst because you believed. Why are you exchanging this beautiful life for a gospel that is actually no Gospel at all?"

The Benefit of False Teaching

Let me say parenthetically that, as strange as it sounds, I am grateful for these false teachers, because they resulted in one of the most important letters in the whole New Testament. More correctly, I am thankful to God who used this error to reveal truth. This is the case throughout the history of the Church; the development of some of the church's greatest doctrines comes from having to deal with heresy, including many variations of the "Jesus-plus-something" lie which tend to crop up in every generation.

This is not to imply that false teaching is in any way God's will. God does not use heresy in order to bring truth. However, as Paul stated in Romans 8:28, "…we know that in all things God works for the good of those who love him, who have been called according to his purpose." God takes the heresies of man and uses men like Paul to confront them, and in so doing reinforce His truth; it is for the faithfulness of God that I am truly grateful.

Over the years, I have had to think through these issues in responding to the legalism, class consciousness, elitism, and Jesus-plus-religiosity that has passed through the church movements with which I have been involved. I have been forced to go back to the bare-bones text of the New Testament, and as a result have come to a deeper and more profound understanding of the Gospel of God's grace and a more profound appreciation for the spectacular and radical nature of God's love for us.

There really is nothing new under the sun. We are dealing today with the same issues that Paul was dealing with then—the same issues that church has always dealt with. We cannot for a second take the radical nature of the Gospel for granted. For this reason, the book of Galatians is as valuable and relevant to us today as it was in the first century.

In Galatians 1:8, 9 we see how serious Paul thinks this issue is:

> But even if we or an angel from heaven should preach a gospel other than the one we preached to you, let him be eternally condemned! As we have already said, so now I say again: if anybody is preaching to you the Gospel other than what you accepted, let him be eternally condemned!

In language that most pastors today would not dare use, Paul makes it clear that he is willing to sacrifice everything for the sake of maintaining the purity and radical nature of the Gospel, because this is a life-and-death issue. Even if a bona fide emissary from Heaven comes teaching a message different than that which Paul taught, don't believe him, and in fact, tell him to go to hell. Can you imagine telling any preacher that? But Paul makes it clear: If some other spiritual authority shows up, even a well-known, respected preacher or pastor or prophet or pope who preaches a Jesus-plus-something gospel, he should be eternally condemned (i.e. damned)!

We don't talk like that very much anymore as it goes against our modern sensibilities, where grace is defined as tolerance. We say we "give people grace," when what we really mean is that we let some issue slide. I [Alden] once heard a radio preacher use Paul's letter to the Galatians to preach on how to resolve conflict. However, if you read through Galatians, you will see that Paul wasn't necessarily interested in resolving conflict—he was creating conflict! Paul's primary concerns were preserving the truth of the Gospel and setting the Galatians free from the legalistic trap in which they had been caught.

There has much shallow and simplistic talk in recent years about unity in the body of Christ and how we shouldn't criticize other Christians. Certainly we are supposed to love one another. It is one thing to love one another, but it is another thing entirely to allow perversions of the Gospel to exist. When it came to the purity of the Gospel, Paul was willing to be divisive. Of course, he was only recognizing that it is the Gospel itself which is divisive. If someone is preaching a non-gospel, it is *they* who are divisive. In other words, they are *heretics*, and Paul has no problem taking what appears to be a divisive stand against them: "Even if I personally (the one who planted this church) should come and undermine the gospel you first received, let me be eternally condemned. Have nothing to do with me!" He is willing to sacrifice everything else—every relationship, every concept, everything—but he will *not* give up the free grace of God through Jesus Christ and the power of the Holy Spirit.

The Desertion of the Gospel

Once we understand what distinguishes the true Gospel from the impostors, we can begin to understand Paul's utter frustration and bewilderment at the desertion of the Galatians:

> I am astonished that you are so quickly deserting the one who called you by the grace of Christ and are turning to a different gospel—which is really no gospel at all. (Gal. 1:6,7a)

The Gospel is simply that God loves you and accepts you exactly as you are, through the perfect life and the perfect performance of Jesus. We are not "good Christians" because of anything we do; we are good Christians because of what Christ has done. Jesus has been judged one hundred percent successful in fulfilling the Law, and that's credited to you and me as our perfection. That is the Good News. God has assured you of life before death and promised you eternal life after death through the resurrection of his Son. Everything has come to you through his Son; all you do to experience this is to act on what you believe.

Why would anyone trade this Gospel for religion? Why would we say, "Really, I'd rather not have life for free; I want to pay for it?" Why would we say, "I don't want life as a free gift through Jesus Christ, I want to depend upon myself. I want to expend some self-effort to get life?" In brief, why would we, along with the Galatians, so quickly desert the good news and the One through whom it came?

The question is even more critical when we examine closely the specific wording of verse six. Paul is not talking about deserting a theological idea or changing your mind about something—he is talking to us about deserting the *One* who called us. Other translations read, "... you are so quickly deserting *He* who called you by grace" or, "Why do you so quickly desert *God* who called you by grace?" When we turn away from the good news, we don't turn away from an idea, we turn away from the person of God. You desert the One because, as it turns out, the good news is not an idea, but a person! When you turn your back on the good news, you turn your back on the person who *is* the good news: Jesus.

We have all done this to one degree or another, so please don't spend a lot of time condemning yourself. Just be sure of this: Even though we have deserted him, God has never and will never desert us. The Hound of Heaven will be baying at our souls forever. Once you have committed your life into God's care, He does not desert you, even though, through falling into religion, you desert Him.

The point here is that we all relate to this issue; this is not merely an objective study of some people's past failings. The motivations, causes, reasons and temptations that may have been responsible for moving the Galatians away from God and the Good News into religious striving are the same things that tempt us as well. Learning this will make us wiser; it will keep us focused on the person who *is* the Good News, and to enable us to not only keep ourselves from this error, but to help others who have been led astray by spurious gospels.

The Problem with Renewal Movements

As tangential as this might seem, I am going to briefly explore the nature of renewal movements and their common fate. In doing so, we can see some of the powerful forces that move us away from God's free grace into the control and structures of religion and law.

Renewal movements such as the Pentecostal revival, the Charismatic renewal, and the Jesus People movement began with God reaching down and sovereignly deciding to pour His grace and power on a group of people who were essentially losers, often both spiritually and morally. They were the kinds of people that Jesus talked about in his Sermon on the Mount: the poor in spirit, the mourners, the persecuted, those who hungered for righteousness, and so on. And guess what? The Kingdom came to them. This is typical of God.

The choosing and empowering of Israel is a prime example: God overlooked the beauty of Assyria, the wonders of Babylon, the genius, power, dignity and culture of Egypt, looking instead to Abram and his descendants. To these He said, "I want you. You're going to be mine." The Israelites, like many other groups that God has chosen, were idolatrous, morally corrupt, and given the least opportunity they would fall into idolatry and sin. During their time in Egypt they had become the poorest of the poor, the slaves, the working class. They did not deserve to receive anything they received, and that is probably why they got it. That is the nature of grace, and why we respond to grace with gratitude. Sinners know they don't deserve salvation; this is the reason it is called the good news.

One of the problems with these "losers" that God tends to choose is that they have no independent ability to make themselves righteous; therefore God's grace is all the more obvious. The problem with God choosing these kinds of people (from our perspective) is that they are generally a messy bunch. We just have to follow the history of Israel to see this. However, God in His grace continues to give grace to those who don't deserve it.

When God touches a group of losers and graciously frees and empowers them, they spontaneously begin to evangelize, often producing great social change as well as growth for the Church. These renewal groups are initially characterized by deep appreciation of God's mercy and grace. They are always asking, "Why me? Why us? Why does He love us? Why did He give this to us?" They never get over the wonder of God choosing them. Ex-slave trader John Newton's famous words, "Amazing grace, how sweet the sound that saved a wretch like me" epitomize this emotional response. At this point in their spiritual journey, the newly saved appear totally locked into grace.

Curiously, renewal movements only have an effective life span of perhaps a decade. I don't know why, but that's what church history reveals: The power, joy, and deep appreciation of God's grace lasts only for a short while. Somewhere around the ten-year mark, religion shows up. It comes in different forms, but when it comes, it suppresses this life, joy, grace, and spontaneity.

One common scenario is this: One or more of the leaders—who enjoyed the abundant freedom of God's grace, become trusted by other people, and as a result of being elevated to a position of authority, become undermined by their own desires. They begin to misuse their authority, freedom, and grace by sinning big, usually involving sex, money, or power. The rest of the leaders then recoil in shock, or at least embarrassment. At the beginning of their movement they had nothing to lose; they were a bunch of sinners anyway. They weren't perfect, but were moving in the right direction. But, over the course of ten years, they developed a reputation that is now challenged by this "discovery" of sin. The movement has become educated and focused on what the Christian community should look like, but reality doesn't match the ideal.

The idea then sneaks in that perhaps grace alone isn't such a good idea; perhaps the Gospel is not enough after all. Maybe grace and mercy ought to be tempered with some rules to bring reality in line with the ideal. Maybe the fundamentalists with all their rules and restrictions had something after all. Grace and freedom (the essence of the Gospel) are no longer trusted and so, as a safeguard, people resort to some form of law and religion. The focus then changes from forgiveness of sin, to sin management.

Paul's Approach

Proceeding through Galatians, we see that the only way to deal with sin is through grace, not laws; Paul never gave anyone laws in response to sin. Instead, Paul said, "Walk in the Spirit, and you will not fulfill the lust of the flesh" (5:16). He always referred to the Gospel, to the reality of their lives in Christ. He absolutely forbade rules and regulations from controlling the Church, in order that grace remains intact.

Martin Luther, as we know, also dealt with the issue of adding human effort to grace. In his response to critics (notably a man named Erasmus) who wanted to add some laws to the message of grace, Luther replied in *The Bondage of the Will* that no man can correct his life on his own, for God doesn't care about any such corrections if they are not done by the Holy Spirit. Luther was saying that even though the outward appearance is similar—the sin may have stopped—it is of no spiritual good if it resulted from human effort. The difference is that on one hand we have the fruit of the Spirit, and on the other, the fruit of human effort.

Paul knew about human effort; in fact, he had excelled in it prior to his Damascus Road experience. In his letter to the Philippians, he says,

> If anyone else thinks he has reasons to put confidence in the flesh, I have more: circumcised on the eighth day, of the people of Israel, of the tribe of Benjamin, a Hebrew of Hebrews; in regard to the law, a Pharisee; as for zeal, persecuting the church; as for legalistic righteousness, faultless.
>
> But whatever was to my profit I now consider loss for the sake of Christ. What is more, I consider everything a loss compared to the surpassing greatness of knowing

> Christ Jesus my Lord, for whose sake I have lost all things. I consider them rubbish, that I may gain Christ and be found in him, not having a righteousness of my own that comes from the law, but that which is through faith in Christ—the righteousness that comes from God and is by faith. (Phil. 3:4b-9)

The word that Paul uses—translated as "rubbish" here and "dung" in the KJV—is only used once in the New Testament. Its primary meaning, by most accounts, is "human excrement." Paul, never one to mince words, shows here exactly how he views human effort, even when it is his own.

It is imperative that we understand that God doesn't need for us to keep laws or strive in order for Him to accept or bless us. Rather, what God desires is our love. Christians who work for God under the truth of the Gospel don't do so to earn points of any kind. They know that their salvation and their continuing relationship with God do not depend on human effort; they work for God out of love and gratitude.

The only way that God can get free love from us is to make us free to either give it to Him or not. No one—not even God—can make us love Him by making us follow rules. What God is looking for is a relationship of love, and that is why He wants grace to remain without any regulations, rules or requirements.

The Galatian "Renewal"

The scenario I have just proposed is perhaps similar to what happened to the Galatian church, since it seems to happen to nearly every renewal movement. It is easy to see how attractive the law is at times—you can imagine how attractive it is to pastors and leaders who think, "Yes, let's have the "free" grace of God, but let's control it a little, too. Let's hedge our bets by having some structure to control people." There is no shortage of seemingly good reasons to add a few rules to grace. I suspect from the text of Paul's letter that these interlopers had some kind of vested interest in preserving Jewish-style Christianity; after all, the Jews had been the chosen people for a long time. Having Christianity without circumcision and the rest of the Law was probably incredibly frightening to them; it represented a complete reversal of everything they had known. I can imagine that for Jews to add a belief in Jesus as God was difficult enough; to say that the Gentiles could completely side-step the Jews and go straight to Jesus was perhaps seen as outrageous. Without Jewish formality, the Gentiles might just run wild. Whatever the specific fears behind their actions, the result was that these Jewish Christians failed to trust the simple Gospel.

By the way, this fear is not unfounded—the truth is, you *won't* be able to control people. Some people will sin and abuse freedom. There will be some who mistake grace for license, and it will cause problems. But, like Paul, we have to sweat that out, because to do anything else would be to deny the Gospel. It would be making the same error that caused Paul to say to the Galatians: "You have denied Him who has called you by grace, and are turning to another gospel."

CHAPTER 4: REASONS WE ABANDON THE GOSPEL

> I am astonished that you are so quickly deserting the one who called you by the grace of Christ and are turning to a different gospel—which is really no gospel at all. Evidently some people are throwing you into confusion and are trying to pervert the gospel of Christ. (Gal. 1:6,7)

As amazing and free as the Gospel is, we have seen how easily the Galatians seemed to have abandoned it to embrace a religious counterfeit which included—of all things—circumcision. Historically, this tendency to embrace legalism has been the Church's greatest temptation, contrary to what you would possibly expect, which would be to move from grace to licentiousness (although that happens, too). Paul was incredulous: Why would the Galatians do this? And, we have to ask as well, why do we who have received the free gift of grace, abandon it in favor of a law-based religion?

Reason #1: Grace is Risky

The first reason we "so quickly" trade grace for religion is that grace is terribly risky; some people will indeed take advantage of grace and abuse it. The Corinthian church is an example of this, and Paul's first letter to them takes them to task for a number of issues, including incest and other forms of immorality, drunkenness at the communion table, snobbery, pride, and infighting (still, as we saw, Paul seems thrilled that at least the Corinthians haven't lost the Gospel). Abuses of grace are generally messy and can result in people being hurt. I should clarify that "abuses of grace" are really nothing more than garden variety sins that happen in an environment not controlled by rules. People will sin whether or not we have rules; however, if someone commits adultery in a church which preaches grace, it is seen as an "abuse of grace" (as if rules could have stopped people from sinning). And as we know, sin hurts people.

Furthermore, abuses of grace are embarrassing for those in leadership positions. When we have been hurt or embarrassed by people's abuses of freedom, we are then tempted to turn from God and His grace to some form of legalism. Religion, with its rules and corresponding punishment for not keeping the rules, seems to offer that which appears necessary to keep sin under control.

God, however, refuses to deal with us on the basis of religion or our performance—He will only deal with us in terms of His grace. Even if we can change behavior through our own willpower or the enforcement of laws, God doesn't care. These efforts are, to God, wood, hay & straw:

> For no one can lay any foundation other than the one already laid, which is Jesus Christ. If any man builds on this foundation using gold, silver, costly stones, wood, hay or straw, his work will be shown for what it is, because the Day will bring it to light. It will be revealed

> with fire, and the fire will test the quality of each man's work. (1 Cor. 3:11-13)

When we turn away from grace to our performance, we turn away from God and disconnect ourselves from Him. Only when we come back to Him personally, on His terms, do we reconnect.

The Prodigal's Tale

There is a great parable that illustrates this, which in my opinion is the greatest story ever told. A young man we know as the prodigal son abuses grace, freedom, and liberty. He asks for his share of the inheritance before his father is even dead, and then squanders it away in the most sinful manners imaginable. Then, only for the sake of self-preservation, he decides that he had better go back home to his father—not for reconciliation, mind you, but only to get more of his father's resources. On the way home he concocts an utterly religious, legalistic plan: Knowing that his father will take pity on him (he at least understands this much) he decides not to try to reestablish relationship as a son, but rather as a simple hired hand. He apparently doesn't believe that his father will either accept him or trust him (why would he?) and figures that he will show his father that he will work for every penny. He has learned his lesson, and has now become "responsible." What he has done is move from looking to his father's love—that is, grace—to looking to his own performance.

However, before the son can even get through his speech his father says, "No, no, no. If you want to come home at all, you come home as my son. Here's the robe. Here are the keys. Here's my MasterCard and the signing authority, the ring." In other words, he says, "Here's access to the other half of the family's resources."

Now *that's* grace. For the father, any relationship based on work and not solely on the basis of love and grace was completely out of the question. Even the son in this story understood that a relationship based on work meant the end of his sonship. What he didn't understand was that his father would refuse to hire him; *this option did not even exist.*

The reason that I cannot relent in preaching this message is because the Bible simply will not let me. This is the message of the New Testament, and to deny this is to deny the Word of God. To accept a works-based religion is an egregious error. Unfortunately, a large percentage of the church is under its deception today. History, apparently, has taught us nothing. We still fall for the same old temptation that tells us that to control people you must have rules—and there is indeed some truth in that! However, God's desire has never been to control his people; His desire was and is to live in a father–child relationship with us, where we are co-heirs with Christ rather than hired hands or slaves.

Reason #2: The Performance Principle

A second reason we may be tempted to desert God and grace and opt for religion and performance is because that is what life teaches us to do. In every other area of our lives, the obvious rule is that if you want something, you must work for it. We are inundated with this from birth. Every day, we deal with a world that says, "If you want anything of value, you must perform." If you want A's in school, you have to meet the required standards. If you want a good job, you have to work hard and do well, and you're constantly challenged to "raise the bar." If you want a nice body, you have to work out—no pain, no gain. There is, as they say, no free lunch.

In every other area of our life, there is a direct cause and effect relationship between our effort and the result; we simply cannot reconcile ourselves to the idea that it just isn't so in the Kingdom of God. In God's economy, you get what you need and want as a gift:

it's free, with no strings attached. This is grace. For some reason we simply cannot wrap our minds around that concept.

And you know, I can't completely wrap my mind around it either, which is one reason why I keep preaching grace. You see, the Gospel is offensive, in more ways than we usually think. We know that the Gospel offends our desires to do wrong, but we don't often see that it also is offensive to our desires to do what we see as good—to earn our way by ourselves. The Gospel reveals and confronts this corrupted thinking.

It is difficult for us to believe that our acceptance by God, while depending on performance, does not depend on *our* performance. It depended solely on the performance of the man Christ Jesus. God's response to our anxiety over this is Romans 5:9-10 (words in brackets mine):

> Since we have now been justified [past tense] by his blood, how much more shall we be [continually] saved from God's wrath through Him! For if, when we were God's enemies, Christ died for us and we were reconciled to him through the death of his son, how much more now, having been reconciled, shall we be saved through his life!

If He showed this tremendous grace to us when we were enemies of His, will He deny us grace now that we want to please him? In our fallen state we were unable to even choose God. He chose us then, by His Grace. Now that we are saved, justified and adopted, God continues to give us grace because *we still cannot perform sufficiently* to earn God's favor. As Paul wrote in 1 Corinthians 1:18:

> For the message of the cross is foolishness to those who are perishing, but to us who are being saved it is the power of God.

The message of the Cross—that we are saved through the performance of one man only—continues to be good news to us who are being saved.

Reason #3: Shame

A third reason why we might turn from grace to religion is residual shame; that is, shame from which you have not yet been healed. Now this is perhaps ironic, since grace is clearly the only cure for our shame. As strange as it sounds, the law, conditional religion, conditional acceptance, and the threat of rejection are all actually *attractive* to our shame. It is the worst thing for our shame, but religion is the thing for which our shame longs.

If we set the performance bar low enough and we score, we get to feel good about ourselves for a while. It keeps our shame and our lack of self-worth at bay for a moment or two. It doesn't cure it, it simply *satisfies* it—temporarily. However, shame is like an addiction; if we keep feeding it by keeping some laws, shame will soon demand that we find more laws to keep so that we can continue to feel good about ourselves. We can never escape this cycle until we learn that our shame cannot be appeased by doing more or trying harder. Shame will eventually overtake and defeat us.

It is easy for a religious system to control someone by making the external requirements (laws) somewhat easy: don't drink, don't dance, and so on (or as the old rhyme goes, "Don't drink, don't chew, and don't run with those who do"). If there are enough rules, people can keep some but not all of them. In this way, there is a little success, which appeases their shame. There is also a little guilt, triggering more shame; however, it is not enough to keep people from trying succeed in those areas, too.

Laws Are Not To Control People

Contrary to popular thought (the Bible is clear on this point, so it should *not* be popular thought), laws are not created to control people, at least not directly. They are created, in part, to make people guilty. In fact, rather than controlling sin, Paul says the law makes people sin more (Romans 5:20)! Furthermore, if people do not understand the true nature and extent of grace, this guilt will produce shame. As a consequence, and therefore a prime motivator of religious systems, people can then be controlled through their guilt and shame. All that needs to be done to trap people in this cycle is to prevent them from understanding grace.

God knew that no one could ever keep the entire Law (if indeed they could keep any of it). The Law, then, was given so that the Israelites would always know that God was holy and that they were always in violation of the Law. This was not meant to frustrate people, but to let them know that they needed a Savior—they needed grace. The sacrifices, rather than forgiving sin, served as a continual reminder that they needed a better sacrifice. However, when religious leaders and teachers obscure this point—when they teach that obedience results in holiness, for example—they can control you.

Jesus Raised the Bar

You might not realize that when Jesus confronted the Pharisees and the other religious leaders and teachers, he raised the performance bar to an impossible height. If the laws were unkeepable in the first place, they were outrageously out of reach after Jesus redefined them. It turns out it is not enough to keep the laws from a technical standpoint—you must also keep the *spirit* of the law: "You have heard it said that you should not commit adultery. I tell you never

ever have an adulterous thought." "You've heard it said love your neighbor. I tell you to love and pray blessings on your enemies." Jesus set the standards so far above us that absolutely no human can keep them. Jesus made the law an impossibility to force us to look for a savior and find one in Him.

However, religion *has* to preserve laws in order to exist. It ignores the plain truth of the Gospel. Religion says, in effect, "Forget the Bible. Forget Jesus, forget Paul, and forget grace. Instead, follow these laws. In our church, do this and you're okay. Dress like us, talk like us, act like us, don't make waves, and you'll be accepted and even respected."

Shame On You

When you are able to keep the rules (at least the "important" ones), you feel okay about yourself. If you're good at playing corporate games, you will do very well, at least on the surface. However, as odd as this seems, shame demands that we fail. Paradoxically, the threat of failure is attractive to our shame for another, very peculiar reason: *Shame demands punishment*, and we need to have an objective standard by which to punish ourselves. Our human nature feels better if we're doing something to atone for our sin, and we tend to believe that this punishment or atonement will cure our shame; but again, this is cyclical. Shame, then, cannot cope without the law; it says, "Give me a specific thing to feel guilty about."

For several years I [Ken] had bouts of episodic depression where I would wake up at 3:00 a.m. every single morning with shame and anxiety, but there wasn't anything that I knew of that I had done wrong to warrant these emotions. I wished that I could think of something to which I could attach the shame and I almost wished that I *had* done something. That is how bizarre shame is. Religion works for this reason: It not only provides opportunities to feel good about ourselves when we occasionally succeed, but it also provides a reason for condemning ourselves when we fail.

Furthermore, shame loves company. Shame desires that others be condemned as well, so I project my feelings of shame onto you. And if you don't keep the law, then I get to condemn you, too. Now I don't feel quite so bad about myself, because I have just judged you as worse than me. People with residual shame love religion, then, because of this fantasy we create through judging others. On the other hand, if we hang on to grace we don't get to condemn anyone, and we become afraid that we will be the only ones buried under guilt and shame.

Because the Gospel is so incredibly offensive to any residual shame that we carry, it can become difficult to believe that we are loved and accepted by God just as we are, or that others are loved and accepted by Him, too. Nevertheless, this is the Gospel and we must keep reminding ourselves and each other of this simple message. As Paul says in Romans 8:1-4:

> Therefore there is now no condemnation for those who are in Christ Jesus, because through Christ Jesus law of the Spirit of life set me free from the law of sin and death. For what the law was powerless to do because I am weakened by my sinful nature, God did by sending his own Son in the likeness of sinful man to be a sin offering. And so He condemned sin in sinful man, in order that the righteous requirements of the law might be fully met in us, who do not live according to the sinful nature but according to the Spirit.

That says it all.

Reason #4: The Need for Affirmation

Still another reason we turn from God and the grace of the good news to performance-based religion is our need for affirmation, especially from authority figures. Many of us grow up lacking the affirmation that we need from parents and others in authority, and the fact that we are Christians doesn't necessarily mean that this fundamental pain within us has been healed. As Paul implies when he says, "…us who are *being* saved," salvation involves an ongoing process of salvation and healing as well as the initial act of salvation which Christ accomplished on the cross. We are truly longing for affirmation from our Heavenly Father, but most of us do not recognize this fact. I think that for those who grew up being properly affirmed by our parents and others, it is perhaps easier to understand and accept affirmation from God.

But for those who are hungry for affirmation, it is a different story. We will reach out for it, but out of ignorance and deception we will look for it in all the wrong places. Much has been written in both Christian and secular arenas about why people look for affirmation from spouses, doctors, teachers, and of course, pastors. When we do this, we are essentially turning these human figures into idols; we are turning to human sources instead of looking to God as our only true source of affirmation.

On human terms, of course, there are some legitimate sources of affirmation: If you are on a sports team, you look to the coach, who is the appropriate person to tell you how you are performing. At work, you look to your bosses. However, you may also see any of these people as a type of father figure—somebody who can affirm you as a person. If this is the case, then you have problems. The coach, your boss, or your teacher will provide affirmation, but in exchange for the appropriate performance, not because of who you are as a person.

In church, where we should be constantly reminded of God's affirmation of us based on Jesus' performance rather than ours, we are often deceived into seeing the pastor or other church leaders as authority figures from whom we can receive this affirmation. However, your pastor has no basis whatsoever to affirm you on his own; he can assure you of God's affirmation (which he should do), but he has no authority to set any criteria by which to judge you. While a coach has the legitimate authority to affirm you with respect to a certain sport that has an agreed-upon set of standards, *a pastor has no such authority* (we will explore this further in the next chapter).

However, in many cases a pastor will be prepared to give you what appears to be the affirmation you are seeking in exchange for your performance according to some set of man-made standards. Churches, unfortunately, more often than not operate on worldly principles. For the church organization to operate successfully people must perform at an acceptable level, and it is far too easy to fall into a pattern of giving affirmation in exchange for that performance. Those who typically get affirmed by church leadership are the ones who serve well, those who follow directions and do not make waves, those who give generously, and often, those who will support the pastor's agenda. I do not recall anyone being celebrated in a church merely for being loved by God.

The only way in which we will ever be safe from the lure of this need for affirmation, and the only way in which we will be immune to false god-figures who will always use affirmation as a tool to elicit our performance, is to recognize that in the end it simply does not work. The fruit of this false affirmation is not affirmation and it is not life—it is simply burnout and spiritual death. Even if we can successfully live up to these false expectations, deep down inside we will know that we were never really affirmed; rather, it was our performance that was affirmed.

What we need is for somebody to affirm us apart from—and in spite of—our performance. We all know that there is only one place to go. If your father failed to affirm you, don't waste your time going back for affirmation because you are never going to get what you really need from an earthly father. It is actually unfair to your father to expect him to give you what only God can. You may have spent years holding a grudge against your father or other authority figure for not properly affirming you, and in reality you may be the one who sinned against them by holding them to an inappropriate standard.

For the short time that my [Ken] own father was around, he was quite abusive. He not only failed to affirm me, he undermined any sense of affirmation I might have had in quite specific and direct ways. As a result I grew up lacking affirmation, but I denied the pain of this reality for years after becoming a Christian. I thought, "Well, I guess I'm just one of those cool, tough, independent people that don't need a father—because I sure don't miss him!"

However, this lack of affirmation would trip me up over and over again. I would find myself doing various things merely to gain affirmation. I'm sure that I even did some things in ministry for that reason, and it's possible, though I'm blind to it, that there are some things I still do today for this reason. But I finally admitted that what I needed was the affirmation of God the Father. I saw that all who were in an apparent position to affirm me were powerless to do so. Even if they had wanted to, they couldn't! If I was going to be affirmed, there was only one place that I could turn. That, of course, was to God the Father, who is the only safe and valid source of affirmation.

God the Father will affirm you irrespective of your performance.

This is what God the Father did for the Lord Jesus Christ at his baptism. Prior to Jesus performing any miracles whatsoever, and prior to his preaching any sermons—way before any performance on Jesus' part except his being baptized—God the Father said to Jesus, "You are my beloved Son, in you I am already pleased (my paraphrase)."

Now, because of Jesus' performance, you and I can receive that same affirmation. I went from someone who denied that he needed affirmation, to somebody who needed it and didn't know where to get, to somebody who has been affirmed by God. And this is not merely a one-time event; God's affirmation is continual. This is not only a *possibility* for every Christian; this is our *birthright.* We get this miraculous affirmation merely because we are children of God the perfect Father.

As a Christian, you have received and are receiving affirmation from God; however because of the some of the things we have talked about you may fail to recognize it, or may misinterpret it. If we are dealing with shame and feelings that somehow we do not deserve God's affirmation, or if we have been conditioned to believe that all affirmation is a result of our performance, we may erroneously draw the conclusion that God's affirmation is a result of our performance. This, then, could trigger a "do more, try harder" mentality, which just spells disaster. This is one reason why we need to constantly be reinforcing the Gospel in ourselves and in each other. We are forgiven, we are accepted, and we are affirmed without any regard to our own performance.

Reason #5: It's Just Too Good to be True

A final reason we are tempted to desert God and the lavish, generous, abundant grace of freedom in Christ is simply because it sounds too good to be true! No one trying to invent a religion would ever come up with a concept like this, because people would not believe it. As C.S. Lewis said in *The Case for Christianity*, "Reality, in fact, is always something you couldn't have guessed. That's one of the reasons I believe Christianity. It's a religion you couldn't have guessed." It is much easier for us to believe that we have to do something, no matter how insignificant, to please God. Because the good news is almost *too* good—something we "couldn't have guessed"—we conclude that we do not deserve it.

This, of course, is the whole point: the Gospel is too good for our human understanding of the way things work (which is why we could never have invented it), and the truth is, *we don't deserve it*! This is why Jesus and Paul called their message the Gospel—the Good News. The Gospel is the good news because it is too good to be true by any earthly standards. We can affirm this truth with all our heart, and we can likewise affirm that we don't deserve God's grace. The good news is that we are accepted and affirmed by God anyway, because of who God is. God doesn't *only* love, He *is* love. He can't relate to you in any other way.

CHAPTER 5: THE TRUE SOURCE OF AUTHORITY

Grace is risky, especially from a leaders' point of view. If people are allowed to believe in true grace, they might sin, and they may cross boundaries that the leaders' are not comfortable with. People might start dancing, they may order wine with dinner, and they may stop (horror of horrors!) tithing. There is an additional reason why people abandon the Gospel which is important enough to warrant its own chapter: Many people will abandon grace merely because we are told to by someone claiming authority.

The Authority Structure of the Church

In the church there is a notion that because someone has the position or title of pastor or because they are gifted in some special way, they automatically have some sort of authority. However, as we have seen, Paul clearly states in Galatians 1:8-9 that this is not true:

> But even if we or an angel from heaven should preach a gospel other than the one we preached to you, let him be eternally condemned! As we have already said, so

> now I say again: If anybody is preaching to you a gospel other than what you accepted, let him be eternally condemned!

Paul makes it clear here with this reference to himself that even an apostle's authority rests not on title or calling, but on the Gospel itself. This principle, by the way, does not originate with Paul. Jesus made the same point with regard to the Jewish leaders:

> Then Jesus said to the crowds and to his disciples: "The teachers of the law and the Pharisees sit in Moses' seat. So you must obey them and do everything they tell you. But do not do what they do, for they do not practice what they preach. They tie up heavy loads and put them on men's shoulders, but they themselves are not willing to lift a finger to move them.
>
> Everything they do is done for men to see: They make their phylacteries wide and the tassels on their garments long; they love the place of honor at banquets and the most important seats in the synagogues; they love to be greeted in the marketplaces and to have men call them 'Rabbi.'
>
> But you are not to be called 'Rabbi,' for you have only one Master and you are all brothers. And do not call anyone on earth 'father,' for you have one Father, and he is in heaven. Nor are you to be called 'teacher,' for you have one Teacher, the Christ. The greatest among you will be your servant. For whoever exalts himself will be humbled, and whoever humbles himself will be exalted. (Matthew 23:1-12)

There was a problem with abusive authority in Jesus' day, much like there is in ours. This problem, as Jesus explained, was that the scribes and the Pharisees took for themselves what they referred to as the Seat of Moses. There is some evidence that in some synagogues, there was an actual stone chair from which the Law was taught; whether this phrase was literal or figurative, this was an office of respect among the Jewish people. From this lofty position, they spoke "from God." Because of their perceived position, they were able to easily mislead and abuse the Jewish people, either intentionally or out of error.

There is some dispute about the exact meaning of Jesus' statement, "... you must obey them and do everything they tell you," and much can be said about this. I won't spend time on these issues here, except to say that throughout the Gospel of Matthew, Jesus is represented as being very critical about the Pharisees' teachings. I would expect that the proper interpretation of this verse would be consistent with that attitude. So far as they read and properly taught the Old Testament, they were to be obeyed. However, the Pharisees and teachers apparently tried to retain this authority for themselves, but their lives didn't live up to the spirit and teaching of the Old Testament.

One Who Understood

There was at least one person in Jesus' day who understood the nature of authority and he wasn't even Jewish! A Roman centurion came to Jesus seeking healing for his servant (Matt. 8). Jesus offered to go to his son, but the centurion objected, speaking a truth that, according to Jesus, surpassed anything Jesus had seen among the Jewish people!

The centurion's statement was this: "You only need command it ... for I, too, am a man under authority." Note that centurion's understanding of power and authority was not because he himself wielded it; rather, the centurion understood Jesus' authority because he understood from where his own authority originated. The centurion's authority was not in his title, or even in his sword, but originated from his relationship with his superiors, the Roman state, and his submission to them.

The centurion had grasped the truth that Jesus' power and authority came from his submission to his Father. Jesus himself had expressed this truth on various occasions, but apparently no one else had yet grasped it. Jesus spoke of this so clearly ("I do only what I see the Father doing") that we might wonder how clueless his followers were. However, the reason we are talking about this now—in spite of two thousand years of Biblical scholarship— is that many people today still have not grasped the true nature of authority. In order to understand any leader's authority, whether it is secular or in the church, we need to know the source of that authority.

There is, of course, a type of authority inherent in many earthly positions. The President of the United States has relatively little power as an individual, but because of the authority placed in the position of the presidency by the Constitution, the office of the President has a great amount of authority. His authority, however, flows from somewhere else: the Constitution, and the people. Let a president try to do something in opposition to the Constitution, and we will find that the man who occupies the White House has no personal authority whatsoever. A corporate CEO also has authority; but like the President of the United States, his power comes from the corporate board and charter. The *owner* of a company, on the other hand, has authority because he owns the company. He does not have total authority, however, because he is still subject to the laws of the land in operating that country. When looking at authority, it is important to know where the authority comes from, because every human authority is limited to some extent.

The Church (speaking of the universal Christian church) is different from any earthly organization I can think of, in that no position in the Church carries any real authority in itself. Neither Jesus nor any portion of the Bible conveys any authority to a specific office or title. In the Church, positions are positions of *service*, not rulership. According to the Bible, the only real authority Christians are obliged to bow to and cooperate with is the truth, Jesus Christ, and the truth, the Gospel.

No office or position in the church is an ultimate source of authority; the *truth* is the authority. A man has authority only as he participates in the truth, preaches the truth and serves the truth. Christian authority is derived from the Scriptures. The source of authority in the Church was a major issue of the Reformation; the Roman Catholic Church maintained that the church—meaning only the leadership of the Roman Catholic Church—and the Pope were sources of authority alongside that of the Bible (as it was interpreted by the Pope and the RCC). The reformers' position became known as *sola scriptura*, or Scripture alone, declaring that neither the church, nor the Pope, had any authority except that which comes to them from Scripture.

Our Authority—and Responsibility

The clear implication of Galatians 1:8-9 that the Gospel that Paul had previously preached in Galatia was the truth, and that the Galatians should have understood and obeyed that word. Paul is so incredibly convinced that this is the case that he says anyone—including Paul himself—who comes preaching a different gospel, a gospel that varies from "Jesus + nothing = salvation," is to be condemned. Even if somebody with power and apparent authority, such as a verifiable angel from Heaven, preached another gospel, the Galatians should curse them. Furthermore, it is the Christians of

Galatia (for Paul was not writing to leaders, but to the people of the church) who are to judge and condemn the heretics; and since Paul is talking to the church at large, this applies to us as well. In modern vernacular, when faced with teaching that contradicts the Gospel, we are to tell the false teachers—no matter *who* they are—to go to hell and to take their demonic gospel back where it came from. If you have the truth, *you* have the authority.

According to what Paul wrote to the Galatians, we are to understand the essence of the Gospel (now there's a thought—where have we ever heard that it was our responsibility to understand the Gospel for ourselves?) and judge what we read and hear in light of it. You have no doubt heard that we shouldn't judge others and that grace and mercy means we should be loving and tolerant. Well, let's read this in light of Galatians 1. When it comes to the Gospel, there is no such thing as tolerance; we are not to give an inch. It's Jesus-plus-nothing, or we are to give the offending teacher the "bum's rush." Not only does a leader's authority flow from the Gospel, *so does ours!*

What this means for us is that you and I have the responsibility to get a very clear picture in our mind of what the true Gospel is, so that we can reject everything else. People who are trained to spot counterfeit money are not actually trained to recognize all of the counterfeits; that would be a nearly impossible task. Rather, they are given authentic bills and are told, "Handle this, look at it closely, smell it, feel it, fold it, deal with it, become intimate with it so that you can spot anything that diverts from this." We do not have to understand all of the heretical gospels—just understand the New Testament Gospel and what it means. Become intimate with every aspect of it, and then we will be able to discern and reject anything that diverges from it.

One of the problems we have as Christians is that we have been encouraged to cut people so much slack under the guise of grace and loving each other that we empower heresy. We somehow think that it's our job to extend grace, to "eat the fish and spit out the bones," and that we should let someone else—like the leadership, or perhaps Jesus at the final judgment—deal with heresy. However, this attitude is not found in the New Testament. We are to speak the truth in love, not allow heresy to exist for the sake of love. The current state of tolerance in the church is nothing more than a trap of the enemy to destroy the Gospel. As G. K. Chesterton once wrote, "Tolerance is the virtue of a man with no convictions."

Paul obviously did not fall into this trap, and neither did Jesus. Why, then, should we? If we know, understand, and serve the true Gospel, then we carry that authority—and with authority comes responsibility. It doesn't matter who is *claiming* authority, whether it is your pastor, an angel, or the Apostle Paul. It's the Gospel or nothing, and you have the authority *and the responsibility* to say, "No, you're wrong."

The Situation Today

Despite the clear teaching of the word of God, Christians continue to unquestioningly believe and follow teachers and leaders—not to mention a few self-proclaimed prophets and apostles—because they either seem or claim to have authority. They may hold an office, have a great following, be spiritually gifted, have academic degrees, be charismatic, do signs and wonders, or they may glow in the dark; none of this conveys any legitimate authority. Because they are impressive by worldly or Biblical standards, they are honored, believed, and followed. We look at these impressive people and we say, "Aren't they great?" Then, out of ignorance or stupidity, we believe and follow them without question (or if we do have questions, we keep them to ourselves so as not to be seen as "critical").

This, of course, is the direct opposite of Paul's attitude. Paul did not even hold himself up as the proper authority; he specifically told the Galatians *not* to accept what he says merely because he was Paul the Apostle. Paul's position was to believe the Gospel, and judge what Paul taught by that standard. Or, as he told the Corinthian church in 1 Cor. 11:1, "Follow my example, as I follow the example of Christ." If a man or a teacher serves the truth, then certainly we are to believe and follow their teaching. But know that *when they divert from the truth, at that point their authority ends.*

It was Jesus who first set the example on this issue. When Peter stepped out from the authority of the truth and chastised Jesus for talking about his coming death and resurrection, Jesus immediately rebuked Peter and corrected him (Matthew 16:21-23). There's no room for politeness; this is, after all, the crux of the Gospel.

Don't Touch the Lord's Anointed!

Leaders who try to take authority for themselves, like the Pharisees of Matthew 23, will try to find ways to justify and to hold on to that authority, occasionally by trying to forestall criticism. One way is to misinterpret 1 Samuel 26:9-11a:

> But David said to Abishai, "Don't destroy him! Who can lay a hand on the LORD's anointed and be guiltless? As surely as the LORD lives," he said, "the LORD himself will strike him; either his time will come and he will die, or he will go into battle and perish. But the LORD forbid that I should lay a hand on the LORD's anointed.

No one is above criticism; even Paul stated that he only knew in part (1 Cor. 13:12). However, if a teacher or leader is insecure about his own authority, he will be especially challenged by and sensitive to criticism. A common scenario is that a teacher or leader gains recognition and reputation because of his gifts or personality, and perhaps God has legitimately blessed his ministry. Somewhere along the way, however, a few people recognize that he is in error and confront him as we should, according to what Jesus taught in Matthew 18.

If the individual is a true minister of the Gospel he likely will listen sincerely to what you have to say. This is a common practice in a healthy church, and I have been a part of these conversations, on both sides, many times. However, if a leader is operating on illegitimate authority, what you might hear is, "You had better be careful about criticizing and questioning leadership—the Bible says 'Do not touch the Lord's anointed.'" I can't tell you how many times I have heard this story from people who have questioned church leadership. It certainly sounds authoritative (and a bit threatening). How should we respond to this? We certainly don't want to be struck by lightning!

This, however, is utter nonsense. The phrase, "Do not touch the Lord's anointed," is not applicable to any current situation or with any current leader. Any attempt to apply this passage to a leader today would be comical, except for the fact that it has been believed by and harmed many people. However, many of us are still haunted by the thought that perhaps we have indeed criticized the Lord's anointed, and so may come under God's judgment. If this is you, you are not alone; some otherwise very intelligent people have fallen for this thinking.

The background of this verse is this: King David said what is often rephrased as "touch not the Lord's anointed" during his war with King Saul. While "touch not the Lord's anointed" is often taught to keep us from questioning authority, the truth is that *this passage is not talking about questioning authority at all.* Rather, it is referring to David's refusal to enter into *physical* conflict with King Saul. When King Saul was pursuing David, David had several opportunities to kill Saul. He refused to do so because he knew that Saul had been literally anointed with the prophet's oil, and singularly anointed with the Holy Spirit of God. David knew that he did not have the right to kill Saul. Here is the passage in context:

> So David and Abisha went to the army by night, and there was Saul, lying asleep inside the camp with his spear stuck in the ground near his head. Abner and the soldiers were lying around him.
>
> Abishai said to David, "Today God has delivered your enemy into your hands. Now let me pin him to the ground with one thrust of my spear; I won't strike him twice."
>
> But David said to Abishai, "Don't destroy him! Who can lay a hand on the Lord's anointed and be guiltless? As surely as the Lord lives," he said, "the Lord himself will strike him; either his time will come and he will die, or he will go into battle and perish. But the Lord forbid that I should lay a hand on the Lord's anointed. Now get the spear and water jug that are near his head, and let's go." (1 Sam. 26:7-11)

As I have just said, Saul had been literally anointed with holy oil and had received the prophet's blessing; he was also singularly anointed with the presence of the Holy Spirit. He was the only person in the nation of Israel that had received the Holy Spirit in this way. He was, literally, in a class by himself. That person, whom God had sovereignly raised up, man was not to put down.

David's words have nothing to do with criticizing, disagreeing, disobeying, or deserting Saul. David *actually did all of these*, and did so quite boldly; in fact, David had been quite critical of Saul to his face! In spite of what you may have been told, you will not miss any of God's blessings by standing up for the truth, even if it means confronting your pastor or anyone else who may be claiming to be "God's anointed."

"Do not touch the Lord's anointed" only refers to *killing* the Lord's anointed, and that's the only context where this phrase is legitimate. If a preacher is paranoid to the extent that he thinks he might be killed by someone in his congregation, then he might want to preach a sermon on this passage. In any other instance, it's merely a smokescreen to keep him from being challenged, probably because the pastor is insecure about what he has been teaching.

A third point is that not only are our pastors and leaders anointed, but *so is everyone else in the congregation*. The point of the New Covenant is that we are all anointed now. You can't point to "the anointed" as if he were a specific person in a different class from any other believer—there are no such distinctions in the Church. The word "anoint" as I understand it came from the practice of shepherds who would apply oil to the head of sheep to keep off ticks and lice. It merely means "to apply oil." In the Old Testament, the practice was used to signify the presence of the Holy Spirit, who was not yet "poured out on all flesh" (Joel 2:28, Acts 2:17). Now, however, we have all been anointed and filled with the Holy Spirit. We may be set aside for a particular ministry, but that does not place us in any special class of "the anointed." So, if the 1st Samuel passage has any relevance at all, it is that we should not harm any Christian whatsoever—which is not a bad practice.

Now it's Our Obligation to Read the Bible, Too...

Like David, you can criticize, you can choose not to obey, you can confront, and you can leave a leader if he gets off track, even if he is "the Lord's anointed" or has been chosen for a particular role. People must be naïve, lazy, uninformed, or have simply not read the Bible to fall for this type of manipulation. You can probably tell this kind of teaching really disturbs me. It is not that I do not sympathize with people who get misled and abused; however, I have to say that this also makes me a little angry, because they had access to the Bible all along! They should have read and believed it. It is understandable for new Christians to get taken in by bad teaching, but many, many of the people who fall for it have no such excuse.

In all fairness to those of you are victims of spiritual abuse, let me say that the Word of God is there to protect you from such things. The Word of God is the truth. You need educate yourselves so that you can judge everything—even what I am writing—in light of that Word. This is not just your privilege, it is your responsibility! We can only depend on our teachers so much. Search the Word of God, and also search the internet! There is no end to the resources that are now available to us; which, of course, increases our own personal responsibility to educate ourselves.

God Told Me ...

One more common method used by pastors and leaders to control their churches is using the simple phrase, "The Lord said," which is nothing less than claiming the full authority of God. I am sure that many leaders are sincere when they say this; however, it may be based more in the culture in which they exist than a real sense of God's authority. This is certainly no excuse; it is simply a bit of background on this practice. In many churches today, people who are spiritually mature are expected to have occasional "words from God"—and these prophetic "words" are often considered nearly as authoritative as Scripture.

I cannot tell you how many times I have heard the strangest things spoken after the phrase "The Lord said," or "God told me," only to have it swallowed whole by nearly everyone in the church. I happen to believe that God still speaks to people today; however, that does not mean new truths are being added to Scripture, or that these prophetic words carry any authority. Many churches that practice the use of prophetic gifts use them in ways that are not supported by Scripture: Paul is clear that prophecy is to be received critically, and evaluated *by the people*:

> Two or three prophets should speak, and the others should weigh carefully what is said. (1 Cor. 14:29)

"Weigh carefully." These words are hardly ever spoken in church, especially when a "word from God" comes to the leaders and is then presented to the church. This is not how Paul says prophecy is to function, for as he writes in verse 32, "The spirits of prophets are subject to the control of prophets." Prophecy is to be given to a church in a corporate setting and judged by those hearing it, not delivered to the congregation having already been vetted by the pastor or leaders, merely to be swallowed whole.

I am not going to belabor this point, as for one thing, I recognize that prophecy itself is a debated issue. My point here is not to present an apologetic for or against prophecy, but to show that even in churches where prophecy is accepted, the authority for judging the truth and applicability of the prophecy is not with the one giving it; as always, the authority is in the hands of the congregation, as they weigh all prophecy and teaching by Scripture.

Paul Opposes Peter

Paul himself modeled how we confront authority on the basis of the truth, when he discusses his confrontation with Peter. Galatians 2: 11-14 says:

> When Peter came to Antioch, I opposed him to his face, because he was clearly in the wrong. Before certain men came from James, he used to eat with the Gentiles. But when they arrived, he began to draw back and separate himself from the Gentiles because he was afraid of those who belonged to the circumcision group. The other Jews joined him in this hypocrisy, so that by their hypocrisy even affected Barnabas and led him astray.
>
> When I saw that they were not acting in line with the truth of the gospel, I said to Peter in front of them, "You are a Jew, yet you live like a Gentile and not like a Jew. How is it, then, that you force Gentiles to follow Jewish customs?"

Notice Paul does not say "Look, I'm a bigger apostle than you are. I have greater authority than you." He says, "You're not in line with the truth." In this case, by the way, Peter was clearly the senior apostle (at least by all earthly standards). If there was one single leader at any point in the church it would have to have been Peter. It was to Peter that Jesus said, "You are the Rock, and upon this rock I will build my church and the gates of Hell will not prevail against it (Matt. 16:18, my paraphrase)."

Jesus himself gave Peter the commission to feed Jesus' sheep, and yet Paul felt free in light of the truth—although maybe he felt nervous about it—to oppose this senior apostle and then discuss it in a public letter to the Galatians! In many churches today, that would result in Paul being chastised for gossiping or being divisive. But, on the basis of the truth, he put Peter down. He said, "No, you're not in line with the truth. The truth is the truth, and it's the authority here, not you, not James, not anybody."

The idea that a leader, even a leader like Peter, should be afforded special status is completely alien to the gospel. Of course, if a man or woman is preaching the good news, if they are serving the Church, then by all means support, honor, and love them. Give them double honor, in fact. Just remember that this does not give this servant the right to stand above the truth or above other people; he is simply an effective servant of the truth.

We must, however, be careful in our responses to leaders that we do not ourselves fall into sin. According to Jesus, as recorded in Matthew 18, if somebody sins against you, you first talk to him privately. It is not appropriate for you to be gossiping among yourselves when the guilty party should be the first one to hear from you. This way, if they see they are doing wrong it can be immediately nipped in the bud. If they will not hear you, if they will not respond, then you get two or three others to confront them. If they still won't respond, then you should take it to the church and let the church rule.

One of my goals in writing this is to equip you with the radical freedom offered in Jesus so that no one, not even me, will ever be able to manipulate you. Once you grasp the truth that you are okay because Jesus makes you okay, nobody can ever manipulate you or make you deny the truth for the sake of acceptance. Once you know you are free—once you no longer need the approval of men and women—you will be able to think straight. And, once you are free, you will be able to read the Bible and understand what it says. You will be able to judge truth in light of truth.

As a pastor, teacher, or friend, I do not want the responsibility of having people look to me to tell them they are okay. Besides believing it is wrong, I simply do not want that kind of power or pressure. To be honest, it sounds like a lot of work. I don't understand why any other leader would want to take responsibility for someone else's life! I cannot comprehend this kind of mentality, but I see it all the time.

Who Really Has the Authority?

In reading Paul's letters we learn something very interesting about who has authority in the local church. As I have mentioned, Paul does not write this letter to the leadership of the Galatian church and tell them to correct the congregation. When Paul talks about what we normally consider to be pastoral issues, he does not write to the pastor or the elders. He does, of course, write personal letters, such as to his friend Timothy. Timothy, by the way, does not seem to have been the pastor of a church. It appears rather that he was acting as Paul's representative—and therefore the context for his letters to Timothy are different from his letters that were directed to churches like the Galatians.

With the Galatians, he writes to the people, to the congregation, because they are the ones who have authority and make the decisions. Paul's comments to the Galatians indicate that he presumes it is the people who judge the authorities and their performance, and not the authorities who judge the people. If you want to know what the Kingdom of God is like, take every earthly structure and turn it on its head. In the world, authorities judge people; the Kingdom of God, however, is about the people judging the authorities by the truth. I can tell you from bitter experience that if you are waiting for your leaders to defend the Gospel, it can be a very long wait. You cannot depend on leadership in that way; it is not fair to them, and it is not fair to the church. It is up to *you* to defend the gospel. It is up to *you* to speak out.

Without exception, the leadership that we see in the New Testament is plural. There is no top dog, pastor, boss, or leader who rules the roost. The apostles always appointed elders (plural). Decision-making and power was a group activity. Furthermore, these elders were not in themselves bosses, they were servants. If they were not doing something to serve the church, they were not elders. As Vineyard pastor John Wimber used to say, "Elders are elders to the extent that they are elding." When you read about elders ruling in the church in the New Testament, the word used is "persuading." They led by persuasion, by convincing others of the truth, not by the weight of their position.

The Vulnerability of True Leadership

An experience from Paul's life illustrates that all church leadership, even apostolic leadership, is subject to its people. In the letter we know as 2nd Corinthians, Paul is defending his apostolic authority among the Corinthian people. Much like in Galatia, false preachers and teachers came to Corinth and brought a gospel contrary to the true Gospel which had originally been preached. These teachers brought legalism, Gnosticism and other false teachings to the Corinthians and they tried to spoil and undermine Paul's foundation of grace.

Paul explains that he has authority among the Corinthian church, and that they should respond to his teaching—they should respond to him personally, not to these false apostles—but he never pulls rank. He never says, "I am a bigger apostle than the others, so obey me," or "I have a higher office, so obey me." Rather, he says:

> I hope you will put up with a little of my foolishness; but you are already doing that. I am jealous for you with a godly jealousy. I promised you to one husband, to Christ, so that I might present you as a pure virgin to him. But I am afraid that just as Eve was deceived by

> the serpent's cunning, your minds may somehow be lead astray from your sincere and pure devotion to Christ. For if someone comes to you and preaches a Jesus other than the Jesus we preached, of if you receive a different spirit from the one you received, or a different gospel from the one you accepted, you put up with it easily enough. But I do not think I am I the least inferior to those "super apostles." I may not be a trained speaker, but I do have knowledge. We have made this perfectly clear to you in every way. (2 Corinthians 11:1-6)

What he is saying is, "I may not appear as impressive as these 'super apostles' but I preached to you the true Gospel. Now you're responding to this non-gospel because it comes to you through impressive, authoritative vessels."

He continues in verses 13-15:

> For such men are false apostles, deceitful workmen, masquerading as apostles of Christ. And no wonder, for Satan himself, masquerades as an angel of light. It is not surprising, then, if his servants masquerade as servants of righteousness. Their end will be what their actions deserve.

These false apostles appeared to be servants of righteousness, and they appeared to be more religious and holy than anybody else. They were, however, servants of the devil. Here is the heart of Paul's concern: these so-called super-apostles were very impressive by human standards, and people were tricked into following them and not discerning the fact that they were in fact preaching a false gospel. The real issue was not the super-apostles' appearance, or even their perceived authority that lead people astray to another gospel; the real issue was that they failed to hold on to the real Gospel.

How does Paul get them back, by cracking an ecclesiastical whip? No, though Paul was the most apostolic-minded of all the apostles. He was often writing about his apostolic rank and authority, but he never used it to bring people into line. He never used his position or his office as a way to manipulate people, or even to convince people of the true Gospel. Instead he says:

> We put no stumbling block in anyone's path, so that our ministry will not be discredited. Rather, as servants of God we commend ourselves in every way; in great endurance; in troubles, hardships, and distresses; ... We have spoken freely to you, Corinthians, and opened wide our hearts to you. We are no withholding our affection from you, but you are withholding yours from us. As a fair exchange—I speak as to my children—open wide your hearts also to us. (2 Corinthians 6:3-4, 11-13)

How does Paul get them back? First, by reminding them that he came to them as a servant. Then, on a personal level, he says, "I opened wide my heart to you. Now respond to me in the same way." What he's doing is putting himself in a vulnerable position.

When people say, "I love you; won't you love me back," they expose themselves to the greatest possible risk of being hurt. In a romantic situation, it's the one who proposes marriage who becomes extremely vulnerable; the one proposed to now has all of the power in the relationship. When Paul essentially says to the Corinthians, "I love you, I did not withhold my affection for you. I made myself totally vulnerable to you," what affect did that have? It gave the Corinthians *all* of the power. Now they were in a position of total authority; they could choose to respond or to reject Paul completely.

True authority is on the basis of the truth of the Gospel, on the basis of servant leadership (that is, true leaders are the servants to the rest of the body), and on the basis of the leadership being vulnerable to the people, saying, "I love you. Won't you love me back?" Even in the face of these super-apostles, Paul writes, "God will deal with them. I ask you to return to me as your father in the faith. I ask you to return to the gospel that I first preached to you, and submit again to my leadership because I *serve* the Gospel and you."

It is not only Paul who gave people that authority—so did Jesus. Jesus has taken out of his own hands any ability to manipulate you. He has loved you, accepted you, and said, "You're free. I make you free, and I have destroyed the law. I can never use the law to control you. You're now free to love me or reject me. I have made myself totally vulnerable. I have not withheld my affection from you. Won't you open up your affection now to me?" Jesus calls us to voluntarily follow him, and we have the power to either follow him or reject him.

To follow Jesus is life and to reject him is death, but there is no big hammer hanging over us to punish us if we reject him. Death (and what comes after) is not a punishment; it is the end result of rejecting Jesus, but it is not a punishment. It's like saying, "If you stay on Interstate 5 you'll eventually get to San Diego." It is our choice whether to stay on I-5 or to go somewhere else. Jesus has given us that choice; we're invited to follow him, but we do not have to. Jesus says, "Choose voluntarily to live today by following me, but I will not force you."

The true source of apostolic authority is in the humble submission to the truth, and we have all been given the power—the *freedom*—to either accept or reject it.

A Word on "Covering"

In response to my teaching over the years on the issue of spiritual authority, I have had a number of people ask about various accountability issues, specifically about our spiritual "covering." I guess I should not be that surprised, but I truly am amazed that people consider it reasonable to ask about this; my assumption is that everyone reads the New Testament, and would therefore understand that the whole concept of covering is nothing more than bad teaching—an old wives' tale. At worst, it is a scam—a pyramid scheme invented by insecure leaders with the intent of intimidating, manipulating and controlling their followers. Not only is this concept *not* found in the New Testament, it is in direct opposition to the clear teaching concerning the nature of the Church, spiritual authority, and mutual submission.

For those of you who have been fortunate enough so as to not be familiar with this teaching, it goes something like this: there is a divine order or hierarchical structure in the Kingdom of God. The person or organization over you provides for you a "covering" under which you operate. That covering includes spiritual protection—keeping the devil away from you. The devil will stay away if you stay under the authority or covering of your pastor, elders or shepherds. Secondly, while under this covering, you can experience the blessing or the anointing of the leader that is above you. The key is to stay under the covering—in other words, under the authority (and control) of your leaders.

You cannot find the phrase or concept of covering *anywhere* in the Bible; it seems to have been pulled right out of thin air. Usually people trying to manipulate Christians take a Bible verse or Biblical concept and twist it. But apparently, whoever conceived of this teaching made the assumption that Christians are so Biblically illiterate and willing to be manipulated that they would believe regardless of its validity.

Remember Paul himself said, "For there is one God and one mediator between God and men, the man Christ Jesus" (1 Tim. 2:5).

The concept of covering is in direct opposition to this truth and is placing a man in the role of mediator. We have one covering: the man, Christ Jesus. No other leader can guarantee you any blessing from God or protection from Satan. According to Revelation 12:11, Satan is overcome by "the blood of the lamb and the word of their testimony." Either Jesus is your protection or you do not have any, for there is no other authority to which you can appeal.

We simply do not have any other options. If you want to grow up into adult Christians, get to know Jesus for yourself. If He says, "Follow me with those folks at that church," then that is what you do. And if he says "Follow me with those folk from someplace else," you go there. And if God does not specifically lead you to any particular church, choose one for yourself that believes the Gospel; the church should bless your decision because ultimately you are responsible to Jesus, and to Him alone.

Authority: The Battleground of Grace

If I were to pick my favorite verse in the Bible, I would probably answer with what I believe to be the pinnacle of Paul's letter to the Galatians, Chapter 5, verse 1: "It is for freedom that Christ has set us free." Being that the goal of freedom is to be free, it follows that the forces of hell will be set on putting Christians in bondage, placing the issue of authority in the church on the frontlines of the battle. It is essential that we have a healthy, Biblical understanding of spiritual authority so we can avoid these obvious attacks on the Gospel and freedom. This is not to give us a basis for flaunting our freedom in spite of those who have been called to serve us as leaders, but rather so that we can live in proper submission to Christ and each other for the sake of the Gospel and the Church.

CHAPTER 6: PAUL'S GOSPEL–THE ONE TRUE GOSPEL?

As the Galatians began reading through Paul's letter, I'm sure many of them were asking, "How do we know who to believe? How can we be sure that Paul's Gospel is correct?" Paul must have guessed that this would be their response, because he took great pains to provide the Galatians with three very good reasons for why Paul was so certain about what he believed.

Paul was convinced that what he preached was the one and only true Gospel, and on this he took a firm stand. He was ready to separate himself and from the other apostles and was ready to pronounce curses on apostles and angels from Heaven should they teach some other gospel. He was staking his life, as well as the lives of others, on the assurance that his Jesus-plus-nothing Gospel was the absolute, one-and-only truth; and the Jesus-plus-a-few-religious-laws teaching was a lie. So, in Galatians 1:11 to 2:14, Paul presents three reasons for why he was so positive that he was right about the Gospel.

Reason #1: Revelation

Paul writes in Galatians 1:11-12, "I want you to know, brothers, that the gospel I preached is not something that man made up. I did not receive it from any man, nor was I taught it; rather, I received it by revelation from Jesus Christ." Paul is making an appeal to authority here, and in this case his authority is Jesus himself—the ultimate authority when it comes to the Gospel. Furthermore, he emphasizes that he received this revelation in quite a dramatic fashion.

Paul (then known as Saul) had first been a persecutor of the church. He had tramped around the Mediterranean world with a cohort of soldiers, looking for Christians to arrest, throw in jail, persecute and even kill. On one such excursion to Damascus, Jesus knocks him to the ground, blinds him, and asks, "Saul, Saul, why are you persecuting me? Now stop it! Go into the city, and I will heal your blindness; you will follow me from now on" (Acts 9:4, my paraphrase). That is to say, Paul had a specific, first-hand experience of the grace he preached so vigorously. He had not done anything to earn God's love—he had, if anything, done whatever he could to undermine, reject, and abuse God's love.

Jesus didn't ask Saul, "Hey, why are you persecuting my people?" He instead specifies, "Hey, why are you persecuting *me*?" Saul had hurt, abused, persecuted and killed God's people but was in reality persecuting Jesus himself. Saul was not searching for Jesus, and, according to what we know, Saul had no notion that he actually *needed* saving. He was a Pharisee, and a good one at that. He had the Law down pat, and was committed to it to the extent that the Gospel was offensive to him it justified killing Christians.

You see, Saul had understood one important truth: The Law and the Gospel are totally at odds with one another; they cannot coexist. As in a classic movie western, the Law and the Gospel face each other on Main Street and one says to the other, "This town ain't big enough for the both of us." The only thing powerful enough to have converted Saul from a champion of the Law to a champion of the Gospel was the direct revelation of Jesus himself.

Furthermore, due to the nature of Paul's experience, he now knew beyond the shadow of a doubt that his salvation was not due to keeping the Law or to any other good works. He knew he was saved purely due to the grace of God. This is the Gospel that was revealed to Paul on the road to Damascus, and he knew better than anybody the difference between the real Gospel and a false gospel that involved works.

One of the problems many of us have is that we were evangelized into a church tradition that taught some kind of grace-plus-works formula. From the time we were saved, we were given a list of things to do in order to be good Christians, so we may have a hard time understanding what "grace only" Christianity is about. Make no mistake: Whatever you did when you became a Christian—whether you raised your hand in church, went forward at a Billy Graham crusade, or whatever—the only thing that saved you was the grace of God. You cannot even give yourself credit for making the decision to choose Christ; the truth is, God chose you. Furthermore, the only thing making you a good Christian is the grace of God. If you for one moment think you have done something in order to earn the right to be saved, it's time to repent and let Jesus save you.

Reason #2: The Affirmation of the Apostles

The second reason why Paul was certain of the truth of his Gospel message is because Paul and his message were affirmed by the other apostles (Gal. 2:1-9a). He knew God had chosen him from birth and had forgiven Paul's considerable sins against the Church. He was certain Jesus had saved him by grace and there was nothing Paul could do to earn it. He was absolutely sure of these things; yet, revealing his true humility and sincerity, Paul sought out the apostles to obtain their confirmation and affirmation.

Paul makes a sort of side comment in this passage that is relevant to our topic: "As for those who seemed to be important—whatever they were makes no difference to me; God does not judge by external appearance—those men added nothing to my message" (Gal. 2:6). It has been proposed by some that Christianity as we know it was invented by Paul, who took an essentially Jewish message and gave it a Gentile spin. However, here we see that the original apostles added nothing to Paul's Gospel; no works, no Jewish Law, nothing. While we sometimes refer to "Paul's Gospel," there is no difference between the Gospel as Paul understood it and the Gospel the other apostles were preaching. They heard Paul's presentation and affirmed, "Yes, you've got it." Here we have unity in the Church concerning the message that salvation comes by through grace alone.

This is in direct contrast to the teachers who had come to Galatia and perverted Paul's teaching. The apostles had not added a thing to Paul's message; however, these false teachers *were* adding to the message—they were saying, "Salvation is through Jesus" (yes, good start), but adding, "plus circumcision." Circumcision, by the way, would only be taught as part of the Jewish Law, and not for any other reason (can you think of any other possible reason for talking adult males into getting circumcised?). Teaching circumcision was nothing less than adding the Jewish Law to grace. Any part of the Law—sacrifices, refraining from pork, or keeping Saturday as the Sabbath—that is prescribed as being essential to salvation or holiness is equally wrong.

Paul subjected the Gospel message he had received through personal revelation from Jesus to the scrutiny of the other apostles, and passed the test. These are first-rate credentials, to be sure. Now, Paul adds one more argument in support of his message.

Reason #3: Paul Fought the Law, and Gospel Won

Paul's third reason to support his claim for having the one true Gospel comes from one of the most interesting stories of the early Church: Paul confronted Peter over Peter's fall back into legalism, and Paul prevailed. You may recall the old song lyrics, *"I fought the law, and the law won."* In this case, Paul fought the law, and the Gospel won.

Some in the church today believe that Peter was the first Pope. While I don't hold to this position, I will admit that at the very least, it can be argued that he was perhaps seen as the senior apostle. It was Peter to whom Jesus said, "You are the Rock." It was Peter who had the privilege of preaching the first sermon at Pentecost. I think any reading of Acts will make it clear that, of all of the apostles, it was Peter who was looked to as the leader. But when Peter's actions were not consistent with the Gospel, Paul confronted him. Paul now recounts that story for the Galatians:

> When Peter came to Antioch, I opposed him to his face, because he was clearly in the wrong. Before certain men came from James, he used to eat with the Gentiles. But when they arrived, he began to draw back and separate himself from the Gentiles because he was afraid of those who belonged to the circumcision group. The other Jews joined him in his hypocrisy, so that by their hypocrisy even Barnabas was led astray. (Gal. 2:11-13)

Paul's concern was not abstract theology; Paul saw that Peter's yielding to pressure from legalists was in a real way undermining the Gospel. Now, this was not about circumcision; the issue here was keeping dietary laws—not what we would think of as a necessarily crucial issue with regard to the Gospel. Peter had been set free from the Jewish dietary laws after he experienced a vision; not that different from how Paul received the Gospel message. However, Peter had returned to keeping this portion of the Law because he feared some other Jewish Christians. What was worse, he also influenced Barnabas to obey this law as well.

We may have some difficulty relating to this issue; most of us are not pressured to follow certain dietary rules unless we have certain health issues. However, the issue here could be replaced with any number of contemporary issues: Does your church teach that dancing is wrong? Going to the movies? Having wine with dinner? Are you taught that Christians are under the law of tithing? Are you challenged to obey your pastor, regardless of whether or not he is right? If so, substitute any of these for Peter's issue with dietary laws, and you can perhaps relate better to the Galatians.

This was not a case of accepting someone "of weaker faith," as Paul discusses in Romans 14, even though Romans 14 also concerned those who held certain dietary rules. The situation discussed in Galatians was specifically about Peter, who had experienced freedom and had already affirmed the truth of the Gospel, returning to legalism out of the fear of men. Paul recognized that Peter's actions completely undermined the Gospel.

The difference between the example in Galatians and that of Romans 14 is this: Paul's point in Romans 14 is that if someone has made a decision not to meat, we shouldn't pressure them to be "free" even though we know it is fine to eat meat. It's not a major issue. However, let's say your pastor has not had any issue with eating meat for years, and has in the past taught on the wonderful freedom of serving ham at Easter dinner. Suddenly he bows to pressure from some self-imposed authority and pulls back from his meat-eating fellowship to become more "holy." According to Paul, he's just lost the Gospel.

These friends of James apparently arrived in Antioch acting as if they had the last word on the Law; enough to cause Peter himself to give in to pressure, choosing the authority of these men over his own revelation from God. Once again, in the Church truth outranks position every time. Paul, who was by his own admission the least of all the apostles, confronts Peter—and Peter, the elder apostle, agreed with Paul, giving one more witness to the truth of the Gospel Paul had preached.

We Can Rely On Paul's Testimony

We have seen that the Gospel Paul preached was confirmed by personal revelation and experience, the confirmation of the apostles, and finally, through contention with Peter over his lost grasp of grace. Paul now tells the Galatians, "This Gospel is undefeatable, it's the real deal, and it's the *only* deal." Paul did not budge on the Gospel, and neither should we.

You probably have not had the opportunity to meet with the apostles or win an argument with Peter. Hopefully you have at least had an experience of God's grace. Even if you haven't you do not need to be in doubt about the truth of the Gospel; Paul has already won this for us. Paul expected the Galatians to understand this point, and we should understand this as well. Being convinced of the veracity of the Gospel, you can stand firm against those who would try to subvert it; the Gospel of free, radical grace is God's bombproof reality which has been given to believers.

Be Convinced With Paul

As you read this, I hope you are saying "amen," at least in concept. Yet, there may also be a nagging shame and insecurity at a deeper level saying, "If I am absolutely convinced this Gospel of grace is true, why don't I feel the confidence I ought? Why don't I feel plugged into God? Why do I feel shame in His presence?"

There may be two reasons for this divide. In general, there are two things that can keep you from truly experiencing what you believe on an intellectual level—sins committed against you, and sins you have committed. Failing to forgive others and failure to acknowledge your own sins will allow your head and heart to send you different messages. Now, please understand something: Neither unforgiveness nor unconfessed sin alters your relationship with God; if sin could interfere with grace, no one could be saved. However, sin—done by us and done to us—can result in an internal dissonance, where we are unable to reconcile what we know to be true with what we feel. This is not a salvation or spirituality issue; this is a healing issue.

We can, at least in our mind, be convinced that the Gospel Paul preached is the true and complete Gospel. It's not "soft on sin" or watered-down; it's the one-and-only "official" Gospel. Based on Paul's three points of evidence, we can be sure of this truth: Paul experienced this grace first hand, as have I, and many others. Furthermore, the other apostles confirmed it, and Peter later reaffirmed Paul's *sola gratia* Gospel after Paul had confronted Peter's about his fall back into legalism. Whenever someone tries to confuse you with why you really should add a little legalism, perhaps to become a "stand out" Christian, remind yourself of Paul's three proofs; I can guarantee you that no one can offer any testimony that outdoes this.

As we are now looking back nearly two thousand years since this letter was written, we can perhaps add one more piece of evidence to the truth of the Gospel: In the Reformation, Luther, Calvin, and others fought once again for the Gospel that Paul taught, proving again that salvation is *sola gratia* (by grace alone), *sola fide* (by faith alone), and *solus Christus* (by Christ alone). Armed with these testimonies, we should be well able to stand firm against anyone who would attempt to add legalism to our faith.

If the best we can do at this point is to maintain an objective belief of the truth—that is, believe it in our mind, if not in our heart—then let us constantly remind ourselves of this Gospel, and make a point to constantly "evangelize" each other. Eventually, with the help of the Holy Spirit, we can also know this truth in our hearts.

CHAPTER 7: PETER AND PAUL–CONFRONTATION AND REASONS WHY

Reading Paul's account of his confrontation with Peter in Galatians 2 raises a number of questions: Why did Peter deny the very Gospel that he had taught and defended? Why did Peter need Paul to save him from his error? And, why did Paul feel such an urgent need to correct Peter? First, however, we'll consider the general question of confrontation in a church setting: To confront, or not to confront, and at what cost?

The Importance of Confrontation

If you've been in a church for any length of time, you have probably learned that confrontation is one of the most socially unacceptable things you can do. In reality, and from a Scriptural standpoint, it can be one of the best things you can do if done in love. However, even when necessary, it can be quite dangerous from a social perspective. Confrontation is risky, and sometimes it can be painful and unpleasant. It tests and threatens relationships and corporate solidarity and challenges the "it's nice to be nice" doctrine. "Getting along"—now called "tolerance"—seems to be among the highest values in most churches. As a result, when confrontation happens it is terrifying, threatening, and often painful. Still, for a healthy church it is absolutely necessary.

There are many obvious reasons why confronting someone in the Church—especially someone in leadership—is unpleasant. One such reason is a false notion about what it means to be a Christian. In North American culture the picture of a Christian is rather plastic and pale. Our theory is that it is nice to be nice, and Christians are supposed to be nice (read "passive"). "It's nice to be nice" is as important as the Ten Commandments and the Beatitudes. In many minds, the perfect church is a "Stepfordish" sort of place, all very neat, orderly, and non-confrontational.

However, "it's nice to be nice" is not the Gospel; rather, the failure to confront error for fear of not seeming tolerant is sheer folly. When you have Christianity modeled correctly—such as the case with Jesus and Paul—you see a Christianity which is quite different from this stereotype. Here, we see two men who are full of love, full of compassion, who cared for the down-and-outers, and who welcomed sinners on one hand but on the other confronted *anything* that would keep someone from the love of God.

We are used to seeing Paul presented as confrontational, but not Jesus; however the "meek and mild" character of Jesus taught to us in Sunday School is pure myth. In the Gospels we see Jesus boldly confronting Peter, saying "Get behind me, Satan" (Matt. 16:23), when Peter spoke demonic foolishness. With the Pharisees, Jesus was just as bold—and let us not forget Jesus' reaction to the moneychangers in the Temple, where Jesus became physically confrontational. There is no "meek and mild" Jesus in the Gospels; we see instead that Jesus confronted friend and foe alike, when they needed confrontation. When we have an actual model of what an authentic Christian is, we do not see anything resembling "it's nice to be nice." We find instead that it is right to be true, just, loving, and when called for, bold and confrontational.

The Unity Myth

We also have a false notion of what it means to be in unity. This is too large a subject to properly deal with here, but essentially the concept that much of the Church has of unity is very pale, placid, anemic, and fundamentally false. We tend to think if everyone is getting along we have unity. This too, is folly. The absence of conflict is not the same as unity; and you certainly can't have unity in a church at the expense of truth.

If we are keeping issues hidden or just not talking about issues everyone knows is there, then we do not have anything resembling true unity. Many churches have in essence created a *virtual* reality—one based on imaginary presuppositions. The very existences of these churches are threatened by the truth; consequently, they become opposed to truth. In these churches, perception is reality and unity is only imagined as disagreements and criticisms are kept buried beneath the surface. As long as no one is talking about the issues, they can pretend they don't exist. However, it is only a matter of time before something breaks and people are wounded, or people simply slip out the back door and disappear. Either way, the church loses.

True unity is not threatened by truth but has truth as its very foundation. When issues are brought to light, we then have a chance at experiencing an even greater unity.

Fear of Losing Relationship

Many people avoid confrontation out of the fear of losing relationships. Many people do not feel secure in who they are in God—and if you do not feel secure, then you are going to depend on others to make you feel secure. These people then can and occasionally will control you, because you recognize that if you dare to confront them, they may withhold their approval. This insecurity will set up a pattern of unhealthy relationships; and oddly enough, it seems that the more unhealthy relationships get, the harder it is to risk losing them.

If you do not know and are not convinced of the Gospel, then you can be controlled. You have to be firm about who you are in Christ, and from that position of strength, you can *choose* how best to confront those who require confronting. Do not allow other people to determine how you are going to approach them. Do not allow other people's hostility towards you or the truth make you hostile towards them. We all need to stand in a position of strength from which we can decide through the leading of the Spirit what is the loving thing to do. Because of our commitment to the Gospel, we need to speak the truth in love whether or not we are rewarded for our actions.

If there are issues you cannot talk about with a group of people, if there are certain subjects that are taboo, then you do not have real Christian fellowship. Without truth spoken in love, you do not have unity. You have to be able to talk openly about issues that are important to you and to the church. The harsh reality is this: If you do not have real fellowship anyway, you don't have anything to risk by confronting error.

Speaking the Truth *In Love*

It is important to remember that Paul told us elsewhere to speak "the truth in love" (Eph. 4:15). Confrontation does not imply belligerence, rudeness, or self-righteousness. I don't imagine that Paul was anything other than respectful of Peter. Far too often the Christians who accept the challenge to confront are those who speak out of judgment, not out of love. As important as truth is, we know from what Paul wrote in 1 Corinthians 13 that speaking in love is far more important than speaking the truth.

When True Fellowship Exists

When we develop this commitment to the Gospel and truth and the ability to confront in love, true fellowship happens. Unity is based on our *commitment* to the truth and to one another, not on whether we all agree. It exists when we are free to speak our minds, in spite of occasionally having to confront and be confronted. On the other side of confrontation, when we have openly discussed issues and have agreed on a solution, we have fellowship. This is exactly what happened between Peter and Paul. Sometime after this encounter, Peter wrote,

> Bear in mind that our Lord's patience means salvation, just as our dear brother Paul also wrote you with the wisdom that God gave him. (2 Peter 3:15)

After this encounter, Peter's respect for Paul increased. He refers to Paul here as his "dear brother," as the one who teaches the truth with the wisdom that God gave him. Relationships must be based on truth; the virtual reality and ugly sentimentality of "it's nice to be nice" keeps truth hidden and healthy fellowship from happening.

We can thank God that Paul was committed to the Gospel and did not believe in the "it's nice to be nice" doctrine of sentimentality; if the latter had been the case, Paul would have let Peter slip, and the Gospel may have been lost in Antioch. As it is, however, we have the true Gospel clearly documented by both Paul and Peter, and we can know this with the same certainly that Paul had.

Why Peter Slipped

Now, we can consider why it was that Peter fell into error. Peter had gone to minister to a group of Gentile people at a new church in Antioch. For a time, he lived in the complete freedom of the Gospel, like the Gentile Christians he was with. He did not eat kosher, he ate like the Gentiles, keeping their dietary customs as God had revealed to him (Acts 10). The Gospel had set him free of the Jewish law he had grown up with; there was no longer any rule or custom that put him above Gentiles, and he lived as brothers with the people that the Jews used to refer to as dogs.

In Acts 10 we can read how Peter was set free with regard to both Gentiles and their food by a direct revelation from God: Peter had a dream in which God lowered a blanket that held a variety of unclean animals. Peter recoiled and said, "Oh, these are unclean animals!" God's response was, "Do not call unclean what I have called clean." Peter was supposed to understand from this that the Gentiles were not "unclean;" they were as "clean" (holy) as the Jews *because God said they were.* By this Peter knew he could be friends with these people and share their culture. I think we can also presume from this vision that the food the Gentiles ate was now also proclaimed clean. Peter accepted God at his word, and publicly defended these new Gentile believers in Acts 15:1, 5-11:

> Some men came down from Judea to Antioch and were teaching the brothers, "Unless you are circumcised according to the custom taught by Moses, you cannot be saved." …
>
> Then, some of the believers who belonged to the party of the Pharisees stood up and said, "The Gentiles must be circumcised and required to obey the Law of Moses."
>
> The apostles and elders met to consider this question. After much discussion, Peter got up and addressed them, "Brothers, you know that some time ago God made a choice among you that the Gentiles might hear from my lips the Gospel and believe. God, who knows the heart, showed that he accepted them by giving them

> the Holy Spirit to them, just as he did to us. He made no distinction between us and them, for he purified their hearts by faith. Now then, why do you try to test God by putting on the necks of the disciples a yoke that neither we nor our fathers have been able to bear? No! We believe it is through the grace of our Lord Jesus that we are saved, just as they are."

Peter understood that we who are Gentiles are saved by our faith in the same manner that Jews were saved by their faith, despite their customs and lack of dietary laws. Peter clearly understood and believed the doctrine of God's grace, how neither Jewish ancestry nor practice had any relevance to Christianity. He understood that the Law was a "yoke that neither we nor our fathers have been able to bear." Peter had the reality of God's grace burning in his heart, and successfully defended it against the other apostles. You would think he would be unflappable in any situation, but apparently this was not the case. Under pressure from people who were not even apostles, he failed. He stumbled. He slipped. If Paul had not gone to confront him, he would have lost the Gospel at Antioch. We have to ask ourselves why Peter, of all people, could so easily lose his grip on the truth.

Paul recounts in Galatians 2:11-13,

> When Peter came to Antioch, I opposed him to his face, because he was clearly in the wrong. Before certain men came down from James, he used to eat with the Gentiles. But when they arrived, he began to draw back and separate himself from the Gentiles because he was afraid of those who belonged to the circumcision group. The other Jews joined him in his hypocrisy, so that by their hypocrisy even Barnabas was led astray.

> When I saw that they were not acting in line with the truth of the gospel, I said to Peter in front of them all, "You are a Jew, yet you live like a Gentile and not like a Jew. How is it then, that you force Gentiles to follow Jewish customs?"

When we read this account, not only do we have to question how Peter failed, we need to ask ourselves how we too might be tempted to stray from the Gospel—for when we read a story in the Bible, it is not merely their story, it is also *our* story. We share in the same fallen human nature, and there are lessons to be learned from any historical account, especially those included in Scripture. There would not be any reason for me to write about Paul and Peter if it were merely a history lesson.

It occurs to me, as I write this, that I feel a bit sorry for Peter; after all, his failures have provided some of the best object lessons we have from the New Testament. We have Peter's aborted walk on the water, having Jesus refer to him as "Satan," his denial of Jesus, and now his losing the Gospel out of peer pressure.

However, in spite of his failings, Peter is still one of the greatest heroes of the New Testament. One reason is that he overcame each and every failing; he is, time and again, a great success story. We hear so much about him today precisely because he *did* succeed. Second, as related above, we can relate to him *because* of his failures; he gives us all great hope, as we are all well aware of our own failings. Finally, Peter's story is the story of God's grace. Peter became an overcomer not because of his own fortitude or perseverance, but because he understood God's grace and chose to believe in it, over and over again. As we look into the reasons Peter failed, we can be encouraged that whatever our own story, we can trust in the grace of God. But now let us look at some possible reasons for Peter's loss of the Gospel.

Problem 1: Sin

Peter fell away from the Gospel for the same reason you and I might be tempted to fall away from the Gospel, and why many Christian leaders in fact *have* fallen away from it—simply put, Peter was a sinner. Leaders have the gift of leadership; they don't have the gift of perfection. Leaders—even apostles—are still sinners; we have all sinned and are dependent upon God's grace and mercy. The difference between leaders and everyone else is that when leaders sin, it is often more public, and their sin can impact more people.

James writes in James 3:1, "Not many of you should try to be teachers and leaders because there is a much stricter standard that you will be judged by (my paraphrase)." Knowing that pastors and teachers are only human, we should not be surprised when they make mistakes; in fact, we should anticipate their mistakes. It is sad and hurtful when leaders sin and do us and our friends and family harm, but if we expect our leaders to be perfect, then we are not living in reality. We should not only understand that leaders will fail, we should also be prepared to forgive them, over and over again.

I think we will have to admit, in all fairness, that many of us have been hurt by leadership because we let them continue their error too long before finally confronting them. Many times we let small things pass, perhaps because we do not want to make waves, we need their approval, or maybe because of a leader's track record. For whatever reason, we recognized danger signs and still let things slip by. Eventually, the error has grown to such proportions that even in correcting it, people will be hurt.

I am not, however, talking about harassing your pastor every time he preaches something you don't agree with. There are theological differences of opinion on all kinds of non-essential doctrines, and if you are thinking independently, I can guarantee you will not agree with everything that any pastor teaches. I am talking about those issues that threaten the pure nature of the Gospel or have the potential to cause major problems down the road. Some wisdom and discretion is required, as is some Bible study and perhaps some input from others.

When we do see hints of a potentially serious problem, when red flags are raised, we should address the issues at that time. When that red flag is raised in your mind, it is like having your car's oil light come on; it's a sign that if you don't take action now, it will cost you later. However, when a red light comes on in the car, we don't take a sledgehammer to the engine, we fix the problem. Likewise, we need to approach our leaders in a spirit of love, gentleness, and humility with the goal of building up, not tearing down. It is helpful, I think, to keep in mind Jesus' warning that we are all sinners:

> Why do you look at the speck of sawdust in your brother's eye and pay no attention to the plank in your own eye? How can you say to your brother, 'Let me take the speck out of your eye,' when all the time there is a plank in your own eye? (Matt. 7:3, 4)

What goes for leaders must also go for us: we need to look after each other. We all have these plank-induced blind spots, and we often do not recognize them—that's why they are called blind spots! Blind spots actually work in two ways: they blind us to our failures, and often blind us to our successes. We need to act as true mirrors to one another other and say, "Hey, you didn't even know that you're good at this, did you? Look at this! You're terrific at this!" Here, we are showing each other our positive blind spots. We need to point out these positive blind spots to each other, including—and perhaps especially—our leaders.

After we have built up a track record of seeing positive blind spots, we need to hold up this same mirror and point out the negative, potentially dangerous blind spots. Let people know if they appear to be wandering from the truth because nobody knows how they look unless friends will have the guts to act as mirrors.

A common red flag that is often ignored is the belief that pastors are a special class of believer and somehow above reproof from the congregation. This is wrong—and dangerous—for two main reasons. First, any teaching saying there are "classes" of believers automatically destroys the Gospel and the truth there is only one mediator between God and man. The only difference between a leader and the congregation is that a pastor or teacher will be held to a higher standard, not that they are any closer to God or have any special benefits. Any pastor who sees himself one step above his congregation is already in error, and in a prime position to fall into much greater error.

A second problem with this teaching is that it is self-protective: It automatically prevents members of the congregation from challenging or questioning the pastor. In this kind of authority and belief system, you really cannot win, at least within the system. We have to give Peter credit in that he did not take this self-protective position; he listened to Paul and agreed he was wrong. However, if you are faced with a system in which confrontation is looked down upon, confront the leadership anyway. The leadership may follow Peter's example and listen to you, or they may ask you to leave—either way, you come out ahead.

Problem #2: Not Recognizing the Implications

Another possible reason why Peter let the Gospel slide may have been that he failed to connect the radical nature of grace with everyday situations—a failure in not seeing the big picture, which is not everyone's strength. As we are not told the story from Peter's point of view, we simply do not know. I am merely suggesting that Peter might not have seen the implications of his actions—that by not eating with the Gentiles when the Jewish Christians were present, he was trampling on the Gospel. This scenario is believable, I think, because I am not sure I would have seen the connection without the benefit of this example; the connection is not that obvious. Knowing what I know about Peter, I do not think that he would have behaved as he did if he had seen the connection.

Missing this connection is a common problem today. There are evangelicals of various traditions that are clearly focused on being saved by grace alone, "just as I am, without one plea." However, the Christian life they present is one in which grace is based on works; you may get in for free, but your "ticket to heaven" is often the last thing you will get for free. The Christian life is presented as a "pay as you go" plan, to the point of trying to pay God back for salvation itself. If you want to be respected as a "good" Christian, there are certain religious hoops you have to jump through, such as dressing by certain standards, avoiding certain activities, and so on. You may get saved for free, but it costs you dearly from that point on.

But, because these traditions do not see a connection between their teachings and the Gospel, they look at you like you have two heads if you accuse them of not believing in salvation by grace. But what they have done—as Peter did—is trash the gospel. They are theologically blind to this connection, in the same way Peter was blind to the implications of reverting to the Jewish dietary laws and separating himself from his Gentile converts.

Perhaps Peter didn't recognize the theological implications of his actions and perhaps we don't recognize the theological implications of some of our actions and lifestyles. We need at least a few people in the church—like Paul—who are able to do this kind of theological reflection to keep the rest of us on track. Unfortunately, there are a lot of churches that still frown on "intellectual" Christianity, which just serves to reduce the chances that anyone in these churches will ever dare challenge the teachings of the leadership.

Of course, now that you have been made aware of this connection, there are more of us to raise red flags for others. It is perhaps odd to think of evangelizing—sharing the good news—with other Christians, but that is precisely what you and I need to do. This is a primary reason why this book is being written—to point out these red flags, so you can in turn point them out to others.

Problem #3: Fear

Paul does provide one specific reason for Peter's giving in to legalism: He acted out of fear, as indicated in verse 12, "But when they arrived, he began to draw back and separate himself from the Gentiles because he was afraid of those who belonged to the circumcision group." Peter, for whatever reason, feared the circumcision party. We don't know why Peter of all people would fear anyone in the church. We don't know why this man, who risked his life to preach the sermon at Pentecost, crumbled before these men who were not even important enough to be called by name! All we know about them is that they were associates of James. We don't know why this man, who bravely defended the Gospel so many times throughout the book of Acts and who tradition tells us was crucified upside down at his own request, should have been afraid at this particular time. However, we know he was.

We usually think of the devil's work as doctrinal error or spiritual warfare, but one of the devil's most effective tools is plain old garden-variety fear. If Paul had not been not there to correct Peter the Gospel would have been lost and maybe never recovered with this group of Gentiles. Down through history, the Gospel has been repeatedly lost at various times and places under the bondage of religion because men in key places faltered out of fear. And, seeing what happened to Peter, we can presume that fear is still a very powerful weapon and we are still susceptible to it today. I have watched this very thing happen—men who were once impassioned by the mercy and the free grace of God gave in to politics and peer pressure, losing the Gospel out of fear.

Fear, which makes cowards of men, comes in various shapes and sizes. It is custom-built to each person's weaknesses. We don't know for sure what Peter's weaknesses were, but that is probably irrelevant; the opening for fear will be different for each of us. For example, if you are personally insecure, if you need other people's approval feel okay, then you are absolutely vulnerable to those people. All they have to do is threaten a loss of approval and fear takes over; the mere thought of this can be terrifying.

Interestingly enough, the only cure for Peter's fear was the very thing he was giving up—the free radical good news of the grace of Jesus Christ. If you feel empty, if you feel needy, if you depend on others to fill you up and tell you that you are okay, then those other people can control your life and open the door to fear. However, if you know deep down inside that you are saved and sanctified by grace alone, you may have some problems, but fear will not be one of them. When you are absolutely secure in Christ, you can think straight and you know that in Christ, you have everything you need.

The Primary Nature of Grace: Our Best Defense

It is essential that we see grace as something more than just one of many topics of interest to Christians. Grace is not just what we are focusing on at the moment; grace is not merely a seasonal teaching—it's the essence of *everything* we teach. If you don't understand grace, nothing else matters. If you don't understand that you are completely loved, accepted, and forgiven—without any effort on your part—

then every other cause is lost. That is why this message is called *the* Good News. Furthermore, as I mentioned at the beginning of this chapter, grace is not just about our initial salvation; *it is the essence of the Christian life.*

What the situation really boils down to is this: the good news is that God loves you because He loves you. He loves you because of who *He* is—not because of who *you* are. Your relationships, even your marriage, will be vulnerable if you think other people's love and acceptance depend upon your performance. If you think for a moment that your performance matters, then the love that you want from others is about *your* performance, not about *their* love.

1 John 4:16a-18 says,

> God is love. Whoever lives in love lives in God, and God in him. In this way, love is made complete among us so that we will have confidence on the day of judgment, because in this world we are like him. There is no fear in love. But perfect love drives out fear, because fear has to do with punishment. The one who fears is not made perfect in love.

If you want to know why Peter failed and had to be corrected by Paul, the bottom line is this: it's because at some level he was fearful. Despite what Peter had been through, despite being forgiven by Jesus after Peter had betrayed him, Peter was still vulnerable. Peter failed, Paul says, out of fear. Theology can be corrected and sin can be forgiven; however, fear has the power to undermine your faith in every relationship you have, including your relationship with God. God's love doesn't change, but your faith in that love can.

There isn't anything *you* can do to be loved; you cannot earn God's love, no matter how hard you try. You can't feed the hungry so God will love you, or pray so God will love you. No, He won't—God will not love you because you *do* anything. He already loves you! You can't get any more love than He already has for you. All we can do is simply ask that God will show you His love, and then believe him:

> This is how God showed his love among us: He sent his one and only Son into the world that we might live through him. This is love: not that we loved God, but that he loved us and sent his Son as an atoning sacrifice for our sins. (1 John 4:9-10)

For too long Christians have limited themselves by saying, "It doesn't matter what I feel." *Sure it matters what you feel!* We've already seen that fear can cause problems. What is fear if not a feeling? And what kind of love can drive out a fear you can feel, except a love you can feel? Don't settle for less. Ask God—and ask him and ask him—until you feel it and the fear melts away.

Once you are certain of this Gospel that Paul preaches and are secure in God's love for you, you will be able to add a very important phrase to your vocabulary: "No, I don't." Someone will say, "You need to spend at least an hour a day in prayer," and you can say, "No, I don't. Prayer is a good thing, but I don't have to in order to earn God's favor." If the pastor says, "You need to be tithing ten percent to this church so God can bless you," you can say with boldness, "No, I don't, and Paul says I should curse you for teaching a false Gospel."

If you are unsure on the Gospel, every little weird teaching is going to cause confusion and fear, and you will find yourself doing all kinds of things just to be on the safe side. However as we have seen, giving in to legalism is not safe at all, for then we risk losing the Gospel.

CHAPTER 8: THE HEART OF THE GOSPEL—JUSTIFICATION BY GRACE

We who are Jews by birth and not 'Gentile sinners' know that a man is not justified by observing the Law, but by faith in Jesus Christ. So we, too, have put our faith in Christ Jesus that we may be justified by faith in Christ and not by observing the Law, because by observing the Law no one will be justified.

If, while we seek to be justified in Christ, it becomes evident that we ourselves are sinners, does that mean that Christ promotes sin? Absolutely not! If I rebuild what I destroyed, I prove that I am a Lawbreaker. For through the Law I died to the Law so that I might live for God. I have been crucified with Christ and I no longer live, but Christ lives in me. The life I live in the body, I live by faith in the Son of God, who loved me and gave himself for me. I do not set aside the grace of God, for if righteousness could be gained through the Law, Christ died for nothing! (Gal. 2:15-21)

The above passage summarizes Paul's understanding of justification by grace (*sola gratia*) through faith (*sola fide*). This is the heart of the Gospel of Jesus Christ. If you understand the essence of justification, you will be able to more easily put the remainder of the New Testament teachings in its proper context. By the same token, if you misunderstand justification, you will have very little chance of properly understanding any other aspect of theology.

I [Ken] try hard to make difficult Biblical and theological concepts simple, and I've been told that for the most part I succeed. However, justification is one of those concepts that cannot be reduced down to where we do not at least have to think a little, and it requires us to wrestle with concepts that sometimes seem to contradict one another. If we are going to understand the truth of the Gospel at any significant level, we're going to have to learn how to think through some theological issues. If we don't, we are going to constantly be herded like sheep from one end of the pen to the other, depending upon who currently happens to have the microphone.

Some people become distressed when they go to various conferences and hear this teaching or that teaching, then come home and say, "Oh, I'm all in a dither, I just don't know what to think." Let's get this straight: All you have to do is read the Bible and you should be able to distinguish fact from fiction. This is one of the points of reading the Bible, besides getting to know God. The Reformers included "*sola scriptura*" in their list of "*solas*," which means, "by Scripture alone." That is to say, Scripture is our authority, not the teaching of any particular church or man-made theological system. Some of the Reformers took great risks—and some were martyred—so Christians could actually read the Bible for themselves. Now that we have it, we have no excuse for not taking advantage of such a great resource.

This isn't to say that there's no value in the traditional beliefs of the Church, such as the Apostles' and Nicene Creeds, or in listening to various Bible teachers. If teachers are humble, intelligent, and theologically sound, they can serve to edify the church. I love great Bible teaching. In the end, however, it is you who are responsible for reading and understanding the Bible for yourselves. Otherwise, like James writes, you will be tossed to and fro by every wind of doctrine (James 1:5-8).

The Problem of Sloppy Thinking

Sloppy thinking has possibly caused more trouble and pain than the devil and all of spiritual warfare combined (well, that might be a slight exaggeration). The truth is not "out there," as the saying goes, it is right "in here," in the Bible. The devil, of course, works with lies, and I suspect a lot of spiritual warfare—as in real warfare, not the common hassles of everyday life—is about misinformation. If we get hold of the truth, then we can defend ourselves against the lies. Lies are weaker than truth, as darkness is weaker than light. If we walk in the light and if we have the then we are largely protected from evil and from being manipulated and seduced by all kinds of false doctrines.

We have to exercise our brains, not only to protect against being spiritually seduced and manipulated, but also enjoy and appreciate the life that we have in Christ. Ignorance is not bliss, it is merely ignorance. As we take a look at Galatians 2 along with some passages from Romans, we will think through the concept of justification, the center of the Good News.

Justification Defined

Justification is a legal term borrowed from the Roman law, which in the Gospel context essentially means that we are now "okay." In other words, we are "justified" or "made right" before God. The opposite of justification is condemnation; justification, therefore, reverses condemnation. To compare Christianity to baseball, justification is a little like being safe—we are on base, and virtually untouchable by the other team. In baseball, there are two options for a base-runner: he is either safe or he is out. The same can be said of justification; if you a Christian, you are on base; you are safe. There is now no condemnation—no chance of being out—if you are a Christian.

Let's turn to Romans 5:16-19 and get a quick overview of justification:

> Again, the gift of God is not like the result of the one man's sin: The judgment followed one sin and brought condemnation, but the gift followed many trespasses and brought justification. For if, by the trespass of the one man, death reigned through that one man, how much more will those who receive God's abundant provision of grace and of the gift of righteousness reign in life through the one man, Jesus Christ.
>
> Consequently, just as the result of one trespass was condemnation for all men, so also the result of one act of righteousness was justification that brings life for all men. For just as through the disobedience of the one man the many were made sinners, so also through the obedience of the one man the many will be made righteous.

The "one man" referred to is, of course, Adam. Adam's sin resulted in bringing condemnation to all mankind, as well as to all of creation. This is the problem into which we were born. Every one of us was born into a sinful world, a world that was doomed due to sin. Furthermore, the natural result of having a sinful nature is that each of us has sinned. Therefore, we have all sinned and so are rightfully condemned under the Law. That, as they say, is the bad news.

Verse 16 brings us to justification: the "gift," the Good News. Christ's death for us overturned condemnation and made us justified—perfect—before God. Through Adam we were condemned. Through Christ, we have been justified, and consequently are no longer under condemnation.

Back to Peter and Paul

As we have seen, Peter began with a good understanding of the radical nature of the Gospel. He was actually one of the first to have the truth revealed to him that God was justifying and giving the Holy Spirit to Gentiles, without requiring they follow the Jewish Law in any way. Peter started out telling the Antioch church, "All people are justified and made righteous before God through faith in Jesus Christ alone." Then, some presumably important church officials came from Jerusalem to Antioch where Peter was working with the Gentile believers. Suddenly Peter lost his grasp on grace, and in fear he retreated back to the Jewish Law. It may not sound like much to us, but according to Paul the impact of Peter's actions was to say in effect that grace only partially justifies us, that we still need to keep the Law in order to be fully justified.

We can presume from the text that these Jewish Christians believed themselves better than the Gentile Christians because the Jews continued to add the Jewish laws to the Gospel of Christ. The text does not say they discounted salvation through faith in Jesus alone, only that they were adding the old Jewish dietary laws as requirements to live the Christian life. If you just wanted to be a "common" Gentile Christian—merely a sinner saved by grace—then trusting in Jesus is enough. But, if you want to become part of the first-class, authentic Jewish Christians, then, in addition to mere faith in Jesus, you also have to eat like the Jewish Christians.

Peter and the Jewish Christians apparently withdrew from the fellowship of the ordinary Gentile people who were merely saved by grace through Christ, going so far as getting Barnabas to follow along. Perhaps Peter saw keeping the dietary laws as simply a call to a more holy life (like many spiritual practices are seen). However, to Paul, this was not moving up to the "next step." This was killing the Gospel completely.

Paul writes in Galatians 2:15-16:

> We who are Jews by birth and not 'Gentile sinners' know that a man is not justified by observing the Law, but by faith in Jesus Christ. So we, too, have put our faith in Christ Jesus that we may be justified by faith in Christ and not by observing the Law, because by observing the Law no one will be justified.

In spite of the fact that we can't be even partially justified by keeping laws, we still often try to justify ourselves by doing good works. When faced with Law—either God's Law or one of mans' laws—it is quite natural to see that we do not measure up. We then have two responses: we can look to grace, or we can look to ourselves. It appears to be our default setting to look to ourselves and see that we have indeed failed to measure up to whatever standard has been set. We then try to make ourselves feel better—to justify ourselves—by pointing out what it is that we *have* done right or even merely to say that we *meant* well.

Paul says we need to forget any such thought. We are not justified by our behaviors in the least. Neither our successes nor our good intentions will provide us with one little smidgeon of justification. In fact, Paul knows we still sin, in spite of our justification. Paul continues in verses 17-21:

> If, while we seek to be justified in Christ, it becomes evident that we ourselves are sinners, does that mean that Christ promotes sin? Absolutely not! If I rebuild what I destroyed, I prove that I am a Lawbreaker. For through the Law I died to the Law so that I might live for God. I have been crucified with Christ and I no longer live, but Christ lives in me. The life I live in the body, I live by faith in the Son of God, who loved me and gave himself for me. I do not set aside the grace of God, for if righteousness could be gained through the Law, Christ died for nothing!

Paul is clear that keeping the Law is of no advantage to us whatsoever, in spite of the fact that those justified by grace still sin. If there was any hope at all that we could be justified by keeping the Law, then Christ died for nothing—and therefore justification by grace would be impossible.

Only the Guilty Can Be Justified

Notice how many times the word "justify" is used in verses 15 and 16 alone; you get the impression this is his agenda for this section of his letter. Justification, as we have said, is a legal term coming from the context of Roman law. It was used relative to somebody who had committed a crime, who in a very real sense owed a debt to society of either a fine or imprisonment. Some translations use the word "righteous"—to be made right—instead of justified. If the debt was paid, the sentence completed, then the guilty party was justified; he was made right, back in a normal relationship to society.

In the context of the Gospel, we all are indeed sinners, guilty of violating the Law; we don't have to argue that point. In fact, Paul's point in verse 21 is that even keeping the Law wouldn't be sufficient to make us justified. The Gospel—the Good News—is that grace, made possible through Jesus' death and resurrection, is what justifies us. Nothing else! Our sin has two effects relevant to this discussion: We are condemned by the Law (and therefore, by God), and our relationship with God is broken. Justification, then, does two things: it eradicates all condemnation, and it puts us in a proper relationship with God.

Here's what Paul wrote in Romans 5:16, 17:

> Again, the gift of God is not like the result of the one man's sin: The judgment followed one sin and brought condemnation, but the gift followed many trespasses and brought justification. For if, by the trespass of the one man, death reigned through that one man, how much more will those who receive God's abundant provision of grace and of the gift of righteousness reign in life through the one man, Jesus Christ.

The gift of Christ brings justification for all who were rightly condemned. Our sins—our crimes against God—condemn us and require punishment. The wages of sin is death, and consequently someone has to die. Because of Jesus' death on the cross and our having been crucified *with* Christ (Gal. 2:20), we are now justified, or made righteous. Our debt has been paid, and we are not only okay with God, He has adopted us! Our sins were not just swept under the carpet to be hidden from view; God did not say He will pretend we are righteous though we are not. No, our sins have been taken off the books, so to speak. They are old news, forgiven, paid, and forgotten. This is an objective truth; it does not matter how we look, act, or feel. Justification is not about us, it is about Jesus.

Of course, if you want to enjoy the Christian life, having your feelings aligned with objective truth is necessary. If you understand and believe you are justified, you should experience the appropriate emotional response and be a joyful Christian. Start with knowing, understanding, and believing that you are justified. Once truth is able to soak down into your soul, and you *really* start to believe it from your heart and soul, then your emotions should follow.

Our emotions, after all, do not create reality; they are our responses to what we perceive as reality. Do not base your beliefs on your "gut;" rather, your gut will usually tell you what you already believe. This is why Paul gave the Galatians three arguments for why his Gospel was true; God gave us the ability to reason and understand truth with our mind, and I think God expects us to use it. One of the works of the Holy Spirit is to bring truth to our soul; if you aren't experiencing truth in your soul, ask the Holy Spirit:

> If any of you lacks wisdom, he should ask God, who gives generously to all without finding fault, and it will be given to him. (James 1:5)

With Freedom and Justification for All

Jesus' death on the cross ensured God's forgiveness of everybody's sins; that is, everyone's, everywhere, for all times. It is not merely forgiveness of known sins, or confessed sins, or even the sins of only those who are "born again." God never put any such qualifications on justification. When you believe into Jesus Christ, you are appropriating the justification that has been made available to everybody. As Paul says in Romans 5:18:

> Consequently, just as the result of one trespass was condemnation for all men, so also the result of one act

> of righteousness was justification that brings life *for all men* (emphasis mine).

This means once you have believed in Christ, justification becomes a personal reality for you. You have moved from death to life, from condemnation to justification, from guilty to innocent:

> I tell you the truth, whoever hears my word and believes him who sent me has eternal life and will not be condemned; he has crossed over from death to life. (John 5:24)

You do not have to sneak out of court hoping the judge will not discover his error. Many Christians act like this is exactly their fear—that somehow, there has been an error, and they are not actually justified at all—so they must throw in some of their own effort just in case.

A Knight's Tale: A Parable of Justification

An excellent illustration of this aspect of justification is in the 2001 film *A Knight's Tale*, starring Heath Ledger as William, a thatcher's son who takes on the totally fictitious persona of Sir Ulrich von Lichtenstein so he can participate in jousting tournaments, which are limited to proven nobility. He makes it to the finals, only to have his identity revealed by his nemesis, Count Adhemar. Following the revelation of "Ulrich's" true identity he is arrested and put into the stocks, as he should have been; he was, after all, guilty of fraud.

Suddenly, Prince Edward (son of the King, the Prince of Wales), steps out from the crowd to proclaim that per his personal historians, William is indeed descended "from an ancient noble line," and is then, nobility. If this were not enough, he adds, "*This is my word, and as such, is beyond contestation.*" He then proceeds to knight William under his real name: Sir William Thatcher.

Like William, we are frauds, guilty under the Law, and deserving of punishment. Our accuser reminds us of that daily. However, here is the kicker: Jesus, our Prince, makes this proclamation: "You are noble. You are a child of the King. *This is my word, and as such, is beyond contestation.*" If anyone but Prince Edward (except for his father, the King) had made such a proclamation, William would have continued to live in doubt and fear. However, by the Prince's declaration, *even William himself could not contest his nobility.* This is our case as well. Jesus has proclaimed our justification, our freedom and our nobility, and we ourselves do not have the right to contest it!

We are free before the Law. Not only that—we've been adopted into the King's family, and "knighted" (sealed with the Holy Spirit and attested to in baptism) as proof. The Law has been satisfied, we are declared righteous, we are made royalty, and it has all been done in the open, in sight of our accuser.

The Other Side of Forgiveness

Forgiveness is wonderful; however, there is another side to forgiveness: You need to let everybody else go free as well. After you know you have been forgiven and that Christ died for your sins, the next step is now to forgive everybody else's sins against you.

There may be sins committed against you that for one reason or another you cannot bring yourself to forgive or to let go, and these sins are killing you, literally. Holding bitterness against other people does not necessarily hurt them, but it always hurts you. I [Alden] once had the opportunity to sit in a courtroom during a sentencing hearing. The man being sentenced, who had already been found guilty, had taken advantage of a woman's generosity and trust, had robbed her and had beaten and stabbed her to the point where she should have died. Her face and body were scarred, a constant reminder of the event. The Judge at one point addressed the man, indicating that in all his years as a judge he had never heard of such a brutal crime, and that if it were possible, he would never let the man out of prison.

When it came time for the woman to speak concerning the sentence that should be handed down, she spoke to her attacker. Rather than use this as an opportunity to lash out at him, which he clearly deserved, she forgave him—shocking the entire courtroom. Her reasons, she expressed, was that she had already been a victim of him once, and she was not going to let her hatred and resentment for him rule her for the rest of her life. She knew that to be truly free of him, and free from his actions, she had to forgive him.

This woman knew what many of us never do: Unforgiveness places us in a prison of our own making. When we fail to forgive, we do not just withhold forgiveness from others; we prevent ourselves from experiencing forgiveness ourselves. When we say, "Christ died for all sins," we mean that Christ not only died for your sins, he died for those sins committed against you as well. Forgiveness—that is, Christ's death on the cross—was a single act. If we fail to accept that Christ died for those who sinned against us, we are also failing to accept that Christ died for us! We cannot have it both ways. Consider this statement of Jesus, as he teaches what we know as the Lord's Prayer:

> "...forgive us our sins, as we have forgiven those who sin against us. And don't let us yield to temptation, but rescue us from the evil one. If you forgive those who sin against you, your heavenly Father will forgive you. But if you refuse to forgive others, your Father will not forgive your sins." (Matt. 6:12-15 *New Living Translation*)

We either accept that forgiveness is for all, or we reject it completely.

Many sins are very hard to forgive, and it seems unjust that we should do so; *they do not deserve to be forgiven*! The point, of course, is that we don't deserve to be forgiven either! We don't forgive people who deserve to be forgiven, *we forgive people who don't deserve it.* That's what forgiveness is.

When you forgive others, you say "yes" to God's forgiveness of the world's sin, yours as well as those who sinned against you. This will set you free, and you can finally get on with life. God will deal with others by way of the same grace and mercy he gives to us. Consequently, we can live in freedom from our own sin and from the sins of others, and we can let others live in that same freedom. This, of course, sounds easier than it feels, because our emotional scars are not necessarily healed the moment we chose to forgive someone. However, the decision and act of forgiveness starts the healing process.

Many people find themselves so twisted, damaged, and hurt, that they cannot forgive some sins committed against them; they not only need the help of the Holy Spirit, as we all do, but they may need the help of a brother or sister to be there with them and walk them through it. When we have become free through forgiveness, we can then give grace freely to others, providing strength, comfort and support. Freedom has many benefits, not only for us, but also for the entire body of Christ.

CHAPTER 9: JUSTIFICATION CONTINUED

As a child I [Ken] spent some of my time on my Grandfather's farm in northern Minnesota. One day when we were in the middle of a wheat field, my Grandfather gave me some advice that has always stuck with me: If you are going to be walking fields during fire season, always carry a book of matches; that way, if a fire starts in the field and it becomes so strong that you cannot outrun or sidestep it, start a fire right where you are, and let it burn. Step into the middle of where it has burned and oncoming fire cannot reach you, because *fire cannot pass where fire has already passed.*

When we believe *into* Jesus Christ—and the correct Greek word used here means "into," and not "in" as in "I believe in music" or "I believe in love"—but when we believe into Jesus, actually putting ourselves by faith into who Jesus is, like jumping into a swimming pool, we are placing ourselves into the only place in the universe where fire has already passed. The judgment of God has passed through Jesus Christ and all the sins of the world were rightly, fully, and completely judged in the one who had never sinned. He took the entire world's sin on himself and it was completely burned; sin was completely judged. The fire of judgment has passed through Jesus Christ—Jesus is, then, the *only* safe place to be found. Any time we attempt to place our hope in anything besides Jesus, we are putting ourselves at risk of getting burned. When we hang on to unforgiveness, we are in effect remaining in the path of the fire. The only safe place for us is that place *all* sin has been judged and forgiven: in the person of Jesus.

There are many reasons why Jesus is unique among religious figures, not the least of which is this: Jesus is the only religious leader who ever died for the sins of the world. Not Buddha, not Mohammed, nor anyone else has ever died for your sins, or even made such a claim. However, Jesus claims exactly that; if you want to make sure the fire of God's judgment passes over you, step into Jesus because it is the only place in the universe where judgment has already passed.

The Bible is very clear there is a terrible judgment coming upon the Earth. No matter what your thoughts are about the end times, most Christians and even some non-Christians know a terrible judgment is coming. There is a theological aspect of this judgment; it's called wrath. The wrath of God is going to burn everything not yet judged, but know this—in Jesus Christ you have already been judged. You were totally justified and you are going to be totally saved, not because of anything you have done, but only because of what Jesus Christ has done. This is why we worship Jesus.

The writer of Hebrews put it like this (words in brackets are mine):

> For God's will was for us to be made holy by the sacrifice of the body of Jesus Christ, once for all time.
>
> Under the old covenant, the priest stands and ministers before the altar day after day, offering the same sacrifices again and again, which can never take away sins. But our High Priest [Jesus Christ] offered himself to God as a single sacrifice for sins, good for all time. Then he

> sat down in the place of honor at God's right hand. There he waits until his enemies are humbled and made a footstool under his feet. For by that one offering he forever made perfect those who are being made holy. (Heb. 10:10-14)

Jesus has once and for all made perfect and pronounced right, true, holy, and just those who have placed themselves into him. And, as they walk in this truth, they are actually being purified and made holy in their own experience. In the New Testament, you do not choose between being holy and unholy, or being a sinner or not a sinner; the answer is "yes" to both realities. Are you a sinner? Yes. Are you Holy? Yes. Martin Luther described Christians appropriately as "simultaneously saint and sinner." You have been pronounced completely holy, and you are being made holy because you have already been made perfect.

When you see yourself as God does, in the reality of justification, you are less inclined to sin. And, once you find out sin really is not what it is cracked up to be and holiness is much more rewarding, you get more interested in holy living. The man or woman who thinks sin is interesting and righteousness and holiness is dull has not had enough experience with either.

How Holy Do You Want to Be?

There have been various "holiness" movements throughout the history of the Church, and much is still being taught and written about holiness. But, my question is this: "How holy do you want to be? Do you think you can be holier than God has already made you?" This is really the issue with those who try to justify themselves—they do not understand that God has already said we are holy. Why then try to justify yourself? Paul writes in 2 Corinthians 5: 21, "God made him who had no sin to be sin for us, so that in him we might become the righteousness of God." There is this wonderful exchange that happened on the cross: He became sin for us, and we became righteous and holy. Here is the whole Gospel in one verse: "God made Him who had no sin to be sin for us."

Once again, how holy do you need to be before you can feel okay about yourself? What does having the very righteousness of God do for your self-esteem? Do you feel okay about yourself now? For many of us, the answer is "no," because we really don't believe in our hearts that we are justified or made holy. That is why, in addition to knowing this truth, we should pray, "God, through preaching, through prayer, by revelation, by listening to you in the morning, through ministry, through my friends and church, somehow get this truth through to me that I've been given the righteousness of God."

Knowing we are truly justified this will do two things for us. First of all, it can cause us to be less depressed, for depression often arises from looking to ourselves. Looking to God to make this real in us will allow us to be joyful and will show us our life is worth living. Second, it will make us "better" people; not more holy or righteous, but rather, our righteousness will be lived out. You see, all holiness preaching does for you is make you interested in what you are being told not to do. The Bible tells us the Law exacerbates our lusts and our desires. If we really want to become better people, we need our holiness to work in our lives. We do not work for holiness; holiness works itself out in us. This is the real difference between holiness preaching and holiness living.

Our legalistic attempts to be justified by our religious behavior are meaningless and downright silly. Paul's words to the Galatians can be directed right to us: "Why are you trying to be better? How much holier do you think you can make yourself?"

It is, of course, wrong to think that you could add to the righteousness of God by doing anything—whether by being circumcised, eating the right food, tithing, serving, or fasting. Furthermore, by doing these things we are raising ourselves above people who don't do them, or don't do them as well as us. Paul says, "We who are Jews by birth and not 'Gentile sinners,' know that a man is not justified by observing the Law but by faith in Jesus Christ. So we too have put our faith in Jesus" (Gal 2:15,16a). In other words, he's saying, "We Jews know the Law didn't work for us, so we have put our faith in Jesus alone, like the Gentiles who never followed the Law."

The Law in Context

Although the Law can't justify us, does this then mean the Law is bad, or wrong, or inappropriate for Christians? Please don't get the impression I ever suggested such a thing. I am not, and Paul is not, anti-nomianist; that is, anti-Law. The Law is not bad; rather, the Law is very, very good, in its proper context. The Law shows us the holiness of God, and it is the only absolute standard by which behavior can be judged. However, it is not appropriate for purposes of justification or sanctification. What the Law does is let everyone know they need a savior. We can't be justified by the Law, because this was never the Law's intent—and also because *we cannot keep it.*

I have stacks and stacks of books on the topic of justification, and they all try to make the Law's relationship to it incredibly complicated. Here is a nuts and bolts version: God's Law tells everybody that they cannot keep the Law. The logic should be that we should look someplace else in order to be justified; we need to find another way. So, we find this "other way" in the only one who was good—the only one who kept the Law for us. When people say "Jesus is the One Way," this is what they mean. As Paul says in Gal. 2:19-21:

> For through the Law I died to the Law so that I might live for God. I have been crucified with Christ and I no longer live, but Christ lives in me. The life I live in the body, I live by faith in the Son of God, who loved me and gave himself for me. I do not set aside the grace of God, for if righteousness could be gained through the Law, Christ died for nothing!"

Paul did not set aside the grace of God for the Law. Grace is how we are justified. We were crucified with Christ, and our sins were judged in Christ, through the Law. The fire of judgment (per the Law) has already passed through me on the cross of Christ. We (in Christ) have already been judged! We (in Christ) have already died for our sins, and that includes sins past, present, and future.

When we died on the cross in Christ, we died with all of the "benefits" of death; we no longer have the power, the ability, to sin. This is not a trick of theology, it is merely common sense; dead people do not sin, because they are dead. The life that we now live, according to Paul, is the life of Christ, which means we now have the power to live out the life of Christ, as we are no longer judged by the Law.

When we finally understand this, the horrible cycle of sin, feeling guilty, seeking forgiveness, and then working harder to pray, read the Bible, and get our behaviors under control only to sin some more will be broken. Let us look at Romans 3:19-20 and get this absolutely clear:

> Now we know that whatever the law says, it says to those who are under the law, so that every mouth may be silenced and the whole world held accountable to

> God. Therefore no one will be declared righteous in his sight by observing the law; rather, through the law we become conscious of sin.

In other words, the whole world is condemned because it cannot live up to the Law of God. The purpose of Law, again, is to make us guilty. Paul writes in Romans 7:7-10:

> What shall we say, then? Is the law sin? Certainly not! Indeed I would not have known what sin was except through the law. For I would not have known what coveting really was if the law had not said, "Do not covet." But sin, seizing the opportunity afforded by the commandment, produced in me every kind of covetous desire. For apart from law, sin is dead. Once I was alive apart from law; but when the commandment came, sin sprang to life and I died. I found that the very commandment that was intended to bring life actually brought death.

What Paul is saying here is, the Law is good, but since we are bad, the Law hurts us. That is the cycle. As long as there is a law to which we can be held accountable, we will indeed be held accountable—and we will feel guilty, and be driven to do something to get rid of our guilt. If we perform for a bit, we will possibly feel better (or will at least feel self-justified or self-righteous) for a little while until we are again faced with the Law; then the cycle starts over.

Remember that justification is the cure for condemnation. When you commit a crime, the law condemns you. There is then a cost, a debt to be paid—whether it is to go to jail, pay a fine, or do community service—which then justifies you. The Jewish sacrificial system included a number of sacrifices that provided some short-term justification—not complete justification—as it actually presumed the inability to keep the Law.

Any religious system that intends either to provide for or supplement our justification, or simply intends to relieve our feelings of guilt, is putting us right back on the condemnation-justification cycle. As long as we keep coming up against the Law we are lost in the cycle because, once again, the purpose of the Law is to make us feel guilty. This meaningless cycle is the antithesis of the victorious Christian life. Yet, this is the cycle that many of us have been involved in for years.

Let's look one more time at Galatians 2:19-21:

> For through the Law I died to the Law so that I might live for God. I have been crucified with Christ and I no longer live, but Christ lives in me. The life I live in the body, I live by faith in the Son of God, who loved me and gave himself for me. I do not set aside the grace of God, for if righteousness could be gained through the Law, Christ died for nothing!

Christ has justified you. Now when you sin you don't need to do some good work (penance) to justify you; you need look to Christ who is your justification. This is not merely another "how to live the victorious Christian life" concept, *this is the Gospel*! If we keep looking to the Law, as Paul is pointing out to the Galatians, we are tossing the Gospel out the window.

Romans 10:1-4 says,

> Brothers, my heart's desire and prayer to God for the Israelites is that they may be saved. For I can testify about them that they are zealous for God, but their zeal is not based on knowledge. Since they did not know the righteousness that comes from God and sought

> to establish their own, they did not submit to God's righteousness. Christ is the end of the Law so that there may be righteousness for everyone who believes.

The end of the Law is Jesus. You do not have to come up against the Law and be condemned, because *the law has been ended for you.* Now, as someone who is justified, the Law functions entirely differently for you; it's like reading the law of some ancient civilization. It can no longer condemn you, because not only did you die as far as the Law is concerned, Christ ended the Law. It can't touch you, no matter which way you look at it.

Another way of saying this is in Colossians 2:13-15:

> When you were dead in your sins and in the uncircumcision of your sinful nature, God made you alive with Christ. He forgave us all our sins, having canceled the written code, with its regulations, that was against us and that stood opposed to us; he took it away, nailing it to the cross. And having disarmed the powers and authorities, he made a public spectacle of them, triumphing over them by the cross.

Paul here says Christ has *canceled* the Law. The code—the Law—has been taken away. It is now complete, done, over; it has expired. Jesus has canceled the only means of condemning you. People keep trying to resurrect the Law for one reason or another, but they have no such power; the Law now belongs to the realm of the dead. The Law still condemns the "old man," so to speak, but who cares? He's dead! This means, of course, that the only way the Law still condemns you is if you step *outside* of Christ.

Breaking The Cycle

We do not break the cycle by becoming better. We cannot possibly become "better" enough to avoid being condemned by the Law. Again, the Law is perfect and we are not, outside of Christ. But now, being in Christ, when we are faced with the Law, we break the cycle by saying, "Christ has ended this standard for me," and acting on this truth *by doing nothing*, except perhaps celebrate our justification (which is why we *celebrate* the Lord's Supper). We only have two choices: We either step out of Christ into a religious cycle, or we stay in Christ and proclaim that there is no Law—no tool of condemnation or basis for guilt—that exists.

The Law now functions for us who are in Christ by showing us the appropriateness or inappropriateness of our behaviors. As the line goes from the *Pirates of the Caribbean* movies, "It's more of a guideline than an actual rule." We are perfect in Christ and we are the righteousness of God. The Law no longer functions to condemn us, but it does serve as a guide—a mirror—of how much we are conformed to God's image, and how mature we have become. We can then act accordingly, whether to seek forgiveness and healing, or to pray for more maturity. The Law no longer condemns us, it guides and perfects us—it is a good thing!

I can't state this strongly enough: We are no longer out of fellowship with God because we sin—we are only out of fellowship with God if we are outside of Christ. The Law is not something to hide from. We have only to remember to not seek to be justified by it, because the Law has no power to justify us.

CHAPTER 10: THE KEY TO THE CHRISTIAN LIFE

To me, Galatians 3:1-5 is the geographical, spiritual, and philosophical center of Paul's letter. These few lines summarize Paul's concerns for the Galatians and give us a very interesting—and for some, shocking—understanding of the Christian life: It is begun in grace, it is sustained in grace, and it is concluded in grace, by the power of the Spirit.

This is quite different than what many of us—perhaps most of us—have been taught. The power of the Spirit is the key to understanding the Christian life. The real presence—the Holy Spirit working in us—is the Christian life, according to Paul. He was very concerned that the Galatians remember how their Christian lives began and how they must continue:

> You foolish Galatians! Who has bewitched you? Before your very eyes Jesus Christ was clearly portrayed as crucified. I would like to learn just one thing from you: Did you receive the Spirit by observing the law, or by believing what you heard? Are you so foolish? After beginning with the Spirit, are you now trying to attain your goal by human effort? Have you suffered so much

> for nothing—if it really was for nothing? Does God give you his Spirit and work miracles among you because you observe the law, or because you believe what you heard? (Gal. 3:1-5)

As you can see, Paul is very angry, and many of you might be uncomfortable with this passage for this reason. As I [Ken] preached through this material some years ago, people in my church expressed concern about what they considered to be unhealthy anger in me—and I admit, I do get angry when I teach against heresy and spiritual abuse. Anger, by nature, produces discomfort; it's unsettling, and I think it is designed to be. However, our modern Christian tradition, with its tolerant "it's nice to be nice" theology, has relegated any form of anger to the level of sin. However, anger has its place, even in the church. Paul's letter to the Galatians is a very angry book, and to pretend it's not is to miss the entire point. He is not being merely dramatic; I believe when Paul wrote this letter he was hot, steaming mad, and to not reflect his anger in some way is to do injustice to the text.

We need to understand a bit about anger so we can evaluate whether Paul's anger was unhealthy. One of the most interesting aspects of anger is that it shows what we value, and to what we are committed. Do you get angry about long lines at the market? This shows that our time is important to us. If you are angry about abortion or the starving, homeless children of the world, it reveals your commitment to justice and to those who can't stand up for themselves. The analysis of our anger triggers can be very revealing.

What Made Jesus Angry?

It is one thing to accept that Paul got angry; he was, after all, human and a self-professed sinner. So, let's look first at what made Jesus angry. Reading through the Gospels, we see that Jesus doesn't get angry at prostitutes or adulterers, and he doesn't get angry at thieves; in fact, he chose to eat with them! Jesus doesn't get angry at sinners; in fact, when he is questioned about his chosen dinner companions, he replied, "It is not the healthy who need a doctor, but the sick. I have not come to call the righteous, but sinners" (Mark 2:17).

What made Jesus angry were the religious leaders who held themselves out to be righteous, as shown in Matthew 23; in verses 27-33 he says,

> "Woe to you, teachers of the law and Pharisees, you hypocrites! You are like whitewashed tombs, which look beautiful on the outside but on the inside are full of dead men's bones and everything unclean. In the same way, on the outside you appear to people as righteous but on the inside you are full of hypocrisy and wickedness.
>
> "Woe to you, teachers of the law and Pharisees, you hypocrites! You build tombs for the prophets and decorate the graves of the righteous. And you say, 'If we had lived in the days of our forefathers, we would not have taken part with them in shedding the blood of the prophets.' So you testify against yourselves that you are the descendants of those who murdered the prophets. Fill up, then, the measure of the sin of your forefathers!
>
> "You snakes! You brood of vipers! How will you escape being condemned to hell?"

What appear to have made Jesus the most angry were church leaders who used their positions of authority and power to put religious burdens on the people. The Pharisees and teachers of the Law taught that God's acceptance was based on performance and outward appearance. Jesus also appears angry because the Jewish leaders had created a class system, placing themselves in a higher position than the rest of the people, which was again based purely on outward appearance. Far from being the "gentle Jesus, meek and mild" that we have been taught, Jesus was both angry and confrontational, calling the leaders snakes and suggesting they may all go to hell. (Jesus really said that?)

Looking at this passage tells us a few things that Jesus cares about. Jesus cares about people knowing they are loved purely because God loves them. He's committed to people knowing they are accepted because God has chosen to accept them, and that their good works and their sins are not a part of the equation. Jesus' words and actions show he's committed to stamping out and healing those who have been scarred by spiritual abuse. This is what Jesus' anger reveals; he's against the arrogant and the manipulative, and committed to the least, the last and the lost.

Evaluating Paul's Anger

Paul was angry at anyone who would attempt to add anything to the Gospel of salvation by grace through faith in Christ alone. Tampering with the Gospel appears to have made him quite outraged, as evidenced by him writing, "You foolish Galatians!" He even writes that he wished the people who were troubling the Galatians would not merely circumcise themselves, but would go all the way and cut off their genitals. This would seem to indicate that Paul was more than just a little bit bothered by what these men had been teaching—he was obviously very, very angry.

It might occur to some that perhaps Paul was taking the situation with the Galatian church personally; perhaps he was jealous of these teachers. This, of course, is something to consider, as we all have to question our motives when anger is involved. However, this does not seem to be the case when we consider Paul's other letters. Paul became angry at anybody who threatened the Gospel by adding any human effort. What did *not* seem to bother Paul was being maligned. In Philippians 1:12-18, Paul writes:

> Now I want you to know, brothers, that what has happened to me has really served to advance the gospel. As a result, it has become clear throughout the whole palace guard and to everyone else that I am in chains for Christ. Because of my chains, most of the brothers in the Lord have been encouraged to speak the word of God more courageously and fearlessly.
>
> It is true that some preach Christ out of envy and rivalry, but others out of goodwill. The latter do so in love, knowing that I am put here for the defense of the gospel. The former preach Christ out of selfish ambition, not sincerely, supposing that they can stir up trouble for me while I am in chains. But what does it matter? The important thing is that in every way, whether from false motives or true, Christ is preached. And because of this I rejoice.

Here we see that Paul has every human right to be upset; he is suffering in prison for preaching the Gospel, and he hears that there are people who are preaching the Gospel with the intent of causing Paul harm. His response? He *rejoices*, because the Gospel is being preached, even if the preachers are insincere. We would probably not be troubled if Paul would have been upset, and I still find myself amazed he has such an attitude.

If Paul would have shown some anger or frustration because of what these people were doing, then we could maybe assume his anger in Galatians was perhaps self-serving or at least unhealthy. But, we see something quite different: There is no evidence, either in Galatians or elsewhere, that Paul's anger had anything to do with his own reputation. We must therefore conclude Paul's anger is simply evidence of his strong commitment to the Gospel.

What Paul Valued

Paul's anger appears to be focused on two things: First, he is angry because someone, in Paul's opinion, has bewitched the Galatians. Second, he is angry because the Galatians, whom he had personally taught, allowed themselves to be bewitched. The word Paul uses for *bewitched* is not a figure of speech, it was the word used in that culture in the Greek language for casting an evil spell on someone where they become bewildered or have their very life sucked slowly out of them.

This, by the way, is exactly what religion—attempting to gain some spiritual goal through human effort—does. Religion is insidious; it appears innocent enough, even high and noble. However, once you fall into the legalistic cycle I have already described, it sucks the very life out of you. If you are trying to be righteous through performance, you are cut off from your life-source, Jesus. Works-based religion has no potential to provide life, it can only suck life from you—it's a parasite. The Gospel is life-producing, because it is focused on what Jesus has done for you. Religion, on the other hand, is not about you; religion is always about your performance.

This explains, then, why so many ministers, church leaders, and workers become burned out. "Success" in the ministry is often based on performance—keeping the rules, attending meetings, and never missing a step. However, when you *know* you are justified and sanctified by grace alone, God's grace provides the energy to do even more than you would have attempted under religion. There a big difference between working under religion—working to gain justification or holiness—and working empowered by grace.

Let us keep in mind that Paul is not talking to the Galatians about Judaism; he is not contrasting the old Jewish life under the Law with new life in Christ. Paul is talking about a legalistic counterfeit of Christianity, and he labels it witchcraft. When you see Christians striving and performing with the life sucked out of them, they are not living under grace; according to Paul, they are under an evil spell. Paul maintains the Christian life starts by believing in Jesus and receiving power from the Holy Spirit. The Christian life continues by believing in Jesus and receiving power from the Holy Spirit. The Christian life concludes by—you guessed it—believing in Jesus and receiving power from the Holy Spirit. That is the Christian life for Paul—life which begins, continues, and concludes in Christ by the power of the Holy Spirit.

Defining Grace

A standard definition of grace, dating back to Augustine, is "God's unmerited favor." However, when we insert this phrase in place of the word "grace" in many places in the New Testament, we find the sentence no longer makes sense. Take, for example, Paul's comment in 2 Cor. 12:9, "My grace is sufficient for you, for my power is made perfect in weakness." What does God's unmerited favor have to do with power? The Eastern Orthodox have a different understanding of grace, which I think is more appropriate: "God's power, at work in our lives." God's grace—His powerful presence—provides the power to live the Christian life. Therefore, a life without grace is powerless, and often even worse—it becomes compensatory and controlling.

In the last chapter, I went into some detail explaining the concept of justification, the objective reality that Jesus lived and died for you before you were even born. When you believe into that reality (again, this language is perhaps awkward, but very descriptive—with your belief, you step into the justified life, stepping into that place "where fire has already burned") you begin to experience and participate in the grace-filled life, where you are judged by Jesus' performance, not your own. Justification is true whether you feel it or not.

However, in addition to your salvation being an objective fact existing whether you feel it or not, salvation is also a *subjective* reality that you *can* feel. The evangelical tradition I [Ken] came from—the sort of semi-educated, right-brained, doctrinally precise evangelical wing of the church—was focused on this first part, salvation by grace as an objective fact. However, we downplayed the reality that it was also an experience.

Subjective Aspects of Justification

The Gospel not only justifies and saves you, it *empowers* you to hear from God, to forgive your enemies, to heal the sick, to cast out demons, and much more. What did Jesus ask us to do that we could possibly do on our own? Nothing! The Bible does not tell us to do anything that we can do on our own! We cannot forgive our enemies without grace. We cannot stop worrying. We cannot resist temptation. We cannot even love our friends perfectly without grace! Do not even *think* of making disciples of all nations on your own. It is by grace we are saved, through faith, and it is by grace we can live, by faith.

Furthermore, salvation not only changes your life, it empowers you to change the world around you. The Gospel is about the three things you want most in life: The first is to be accepted just the way you are. Second, the Gospel is also about *not* having to stay the way you are. Grace—the presence of the Holy Spirit—empowers us to change, to become recreated in God's image. As Paul writes in 2 Corinthians 3:18, "And we, who with unveiled faces all reflect the Lord's glory, are being transformed into his likeness with ever-increasing glory, which comes from the Lord, who is the Spirit."

Third, grace also empowers us to change the world around us (Acts 1:8). These are the two aspects of the Gospel, the objective and the subjective.

Now let's look again at what Paul writes in Galatians 3:1-5:

> You foolish Galatians! Who has bewitched you? … I would like to learn just one thing from you: Did you receive the Spirit by observing the law, or by believing what you heard? Are you so foolish? After beginning with the Spirit, are you now trying to attain your goal by human effort? Have you suffered so much for nothing—if it really was for nothing? Does God give you his Spirit and work miracles among you because you observe the law, or because you believe what you heard?

When Paul asked, "Did you receive the Spirit…," he was not talking about some objective, cold, theological understanding of the Gospel, he was talking about something they had subjectively experienced. This is a rhetorical question, because Paul knew the Galatians would understand him. When the Galatians received the Spirit, something subjective happened to them. Paul doesn't say, "Remember when you were justified?" or, "Remember when you asked Jesus into your heart?" "Remember when you came forward?" "Remember when you raised your hand?" Rather, he asks the Galatians to remember when they received the Holy Spirit.

Paul did not expect the Galatians to believe they were Christians based on theology alone; he expected some evidence of justification to be manifest in their lives. We can assume they experienced some of that power when they were first saved. Walking by faith, according to Paul, is not looking back to some point in your life when you made a decision "for Christ." When Paul says to take our Christian lives by faith, he is not saying "don't expect to experience any grace or power." I think this would have been a foreign concept for Paul. What Paul is saying is, "Don't strive; rather, by faith, expect God's power to work in your life." If there is no evidence of the Spirit in your life—if there is no power, no change, no joy, no fruit, no anything—then chances are you are not justified, either. The good news, of course, is that it is not too late; you can ask Jesus into your life, and ask for the power of the Holy Spirit to be manifest, and you can be justified and empowered, right now, for free.

I think one of the reasons there is so little evidence of the Spirit today when someone becomes a Christian is that there is so little expectation; people are almost conditioned *not* to experience anything. Plus, many traditions start loading on legalism from day one, so grace is choked before it gets a chance to take root. On the other end of the spectrum are traditions that *do* require some "supernatural" evidence of salvation, like speaking in tongues. I believe that supernatural gifts do exist, but there is no *requirement* to have them that is shown in the Bible. Such expectations only cause striving, which again chokes out real grace and power.

None of the so-called "evidences" are necessary for salvation; for some, the work of the Spirit is more subtle than in others. Do not ever downplay the objective, bomb-proof reality of your salvation because you simply believe, whether or not you feel any particular way. Having said this, expect to feel. Expect to be changed. Expect the fruit of the Spirit to be evidenced in your life. Do not strive for it, *look* for it.

The Lesson of the Orange Groves

The late John Wimber once told a story of when he was a child in Orange County, California. He would be wakened early in the morning by the deafening sound of the orange trees groaning as they produced fruit. The congregation sat in stunned silence until they realized the point he was making: Trees *never* do this. Trees produce fruit by nature; they cannot help it, unless they are sick, damaged, or dead. Do not strive to produce fruit; rely on God's grace to do that for you.

Paul's point is the power of the Spirit is available by believing. Salvation and right standing with God is yours by believing that Jesus Christ has lived and died for you, and the power to live the Christian life is yours as well. Don't try to change by human effort. You can, and should, *participate* in your Christian life, by fasting, prayer, reading your Bible and so on; participate in the life He gives you, but do not do these things in order to *get* the Christian life. The Christian life you get for free, by the Spirit, whether you do these things or not. The Christian disciplines are not ways of becoming holy or of hanging on to your salvation; they are simply a means of participating in the life that Jesus has freely given us.

The work of the Spirit is also not meant to merely be an initiation experience. The work of the Spirit is an ongoing day-to-day reality. Unfortunately, much of the focus on the Holy Spirit in the church of the last one hundred years has been the sensationalist variety, such as healing the sick, speaking in tongues and casting out demons, and this tends to give the Holy Spirit a sensationalist reputation. As someone who has prayed for the sick, let me tell you this: Healing the sick is easy. Casting out demons is easy. What is hard is staying married. What is hard is raising your children. What is hard is not worrying about money. What is hard is living life in peace, acting with integrity, and speaking the truth in love. These things are hard. A true sign of the Holy Spirit's power in your life is having a good marriage and raising children, not raising the dead.

Paul asks the question: Did you receive the power of the Spirit because you worked hard and you were good enough? Again, this is a rhetorical question, with the obvious answer being "No, you received it by believing what you were told." The point of Paul's question is this: You were given the Spirit by believing, not by anything you did. This goes for salvation and as well as day-to-day living. The failure of the Galatians is while they accepted salvation by grace, they then tried to work for what they already had. They were bewitched. By trying to add performance and works to faith in Christ, the life they were given had been squelched.

The Christian life, as taught by Paul, is a life dependent upon the free gift of the Holy Spirit active in our lives on a daily basis. This is not contingent upon our obedience, or our faithfulness, our ability to keep from sin, or our keeping religious rules and regulations. The gift of the Holy Spirit is free—it was free at the beginning, and it is free now, by believing that it is free.

CHAPTER 11: THE PLACE AND PURPOSE OF THE LAW

For all of the negative attention the Law has received so far, let us make one thing clear: The Law is not evil. In fact, the Bible tells us the Law is good (Ps. 19:7,8; Neh. 9:13). The Law has a purpose and a place. But as we will see, things go bad when the Law is taken out of its proper context.

In Galatians 3:10-14, Paul writes:

> All who rely on observing the law are under a curse, for it is written: "Cursed is everyone who does not continue to do everything written in the Book of the Law." Clearly no one is justified before God by the law, because, "The righteous will live by faith." The law is not based on faith; to the contrary, "The man who does these things will live by them." Christ redeemed us from the curse of the law by becoming a curse for us, for it is written, "Cursed is everyone who is hung on a tree." He redeemed us in order that the blessing given to Abraham might come to the Gentiles through Christ Jesus, so that by faith we receive the promise of the Spirit.

In other words, if someone wants to depend on the Law as a basis for their relationship with God, he or she had better keep one hundred percent of it. The implication is clear: No one can keep one hundred percent of the Law, and so they would be foolish to try; he or she would be voluntarily putting themselves under a curse.

Paul then introduces a new argument: Even if you *could* keep the whole law, you would be wasting your time, as no one can be justified by the Law. Rather, Paul quotes Habakkuk 2:4, "…the righteous will live by his faith." Righteousness—justification—is by faith, and as Paul goes on to say, "the law is not based on faith." The Law is ruled out completely as a source of righteousness, *even in the Old Testament.* According to the Habakkuk passage, righteousness has always been by faith.

Having ruled out the Law completely as a source of righteousness, Paul declares that Christ has redeemed us; this is an objective truth, not subject to our performance. It does not matter whether we feel redeemed or not—for that matter, it does not even matter if we believe it—Christ's redeeming work on the cross is a true fact nonetheless. Paul does not stop here; he continues to say that because we were justified, we have also received the powerful presence of God, the subjective experience of "the promise of the Spirit."

Whenever the Spirit is talked about in the New Testament, it refers to the dynamic, powerful presence of God. We receive the Holy Spirit and grace because we are justified. When Paul talks about the Christian life, he is always referring to both the objective, historical reality of justification and our being sealed with the Holy Spirit, and the subjective experience of the Spirit.

The Abrahamic Covenant

In verse 15, Paul shifts gears and starts to approach the grace vs. law issue from a new perspective. Galatians 3:15 is set up by what he had just said in verses 1-10, especially verses 6-9:

> Consider Abraham: "He believed God, and it was credited to him as righteousness." Understand, then, that those who believe are children of Abraham. The Scripture foresaw that God would justify the Gentiles by faith, and announced the gospel in advance to Abraham: "All nations will be blessed through you." So those who have faith are blessed along with Abraham, the man of faith.

Paul tells us to look at Abraham, because the Galatians—even though they are Gentiles—relate to God in exactly the same way Abraham did: by believing God; that is, by faith. Those who trust in observing the Law, however, are under a curse. Abraham (whose covenant with God predated the Law by several generations) simply believed and trusted what God said as evidenced by his acting on it; and because he *believed*, God ruled Abraham righteous. Abraham did not work for his righteousness, nor did he trust in his own performance; he believed God, and this justified him.

This is how we today are justified. Paul is demonstrating here that the principle of justification by faith is consistent with the Old Testament and is not a new teaching. He is also showing how easy this is—another reason why it is called the Good News. It is so simple that it confounds our twisted, convoluted, legalistic, guilt-ridden, obsessed minds, but the objective truth is, this is how it worked for Abraham and this is how it still works for us. When God says all nations on earth will be blessed through Abraham, He is referring to His covenant with Abraham and the promise of righteousness (justification) by faith. Because of what God promised Abraham, everyone who believes the goodness of God will experience the benefits of a justified relationship. Again, it is important to understand that this covenant—known as the Abrahamic Covenant—was in existence long before the Law was given, and never went out of effect.

Paul, though, still has to account for the Law—this is, after all, the reason for writing the letter in the first place. Jewish Christians, who were perhaps having a hard time making the shift from Law to grace, had taught the Galatians that they could be saved by faith, but then had to submit to the Law to continue on in the faith. No, Paul can't just ignore the Law, and neither can we.

The Jewish Christians' claim that people must follow the Law was a very powerful and persuasive argument. Christianity, after all, was born out of Judaism. Jesus and all of the apostles were Jewish, so they all had been circumcised and raised following the Law. The Law had to be there for a purpose; it could not just be ignored or disposed of. The early Christians, especially those from Jerusalem whose lives were steeped in the Law, knew that the Bible they had—the Old Testament—was the very Word of God, and the Word of God did not change. This, then, raises the question, "If we are justified by trusting in God and not by keeping the Law, why was Israel put under the Law in the first place?" A secondary question, which Paul begins to answer now, is, "If God gave the Law, how can we now ignore it?"

Paul says, in verses 15-18:

> Brothers, let me take an example from everyday life. Just as no one can set aside or add to a human covenant that has been duly established, so it is in this case. The promises were spoken to Abraham and to his seed. The Scripture does not say "and to seeds," meaning many

> people, but "and to your seed," meaning one person, who is Christ. What I mean is this: The law, introduced 430 years later, does not set aside the covenant previously established by God and thus do away with the promise. For if the inheritance depends on the law, then it no longer depends on a promise; but God in his grace gave it to Abraham through a promise.

Paul's point here, which is nothing short of brilliant, is essentially a legal argument based upon the principles of covenants. He explains how God had made a covenant with Abraham about 430 years before the Law was given through Moses. This covenant was given by grace; that is, it was not based upon Abraham's performance, but upon God's goodness. God unilaterally set the terms, but also guaranteed that He would keep all the terms. This covenant also applied to Abraham's descendants, and since the terms were set by God, the covenant could not be altered—nothing could be taken from it, or added to it. Therefore the Law, which came much later, could do nothing to set aside or change the covenant of justification by grace through faith. The Law did not supersede the covenant in the Old Testament, so it certainly could not supersede the covenant in the first century; and if not the first century, then certainly not today.

Law, or Grace?

If the inheritance—the benefits of the Abrahamic covenant—depends upon the Law, then it no longer depends on the promise given by grace to Abraham. However, we find that the covenant is still in effect; the covenant was not made solely with Abraham, it was also made with "his seed," Abraham's descendant, whom Paul identifies as Jesus. In Jesus, and only in Jesus, the covenant with

Abraham *is still current*. The benefits of the covenant—righteousness through faith—were promised to Abraham, and to Jesus. If we are "in Christ," as Paul says we are, we are also under that covenant and have the same righteousness through faith.

To share in the promise of the covenant, we have to either become "in Abraham" or "in Christ." Abraham is dead, and we are not his descendants; therefore, we have no ability to become "in Abraham." Jesus, however, is not dead but very much alive. We can become "in Jesus" through faith, and therefore share in the promise of the covenant, through faith.

Paul has now laid out two options: First, we have the Abrahamic covenant, in which we have righteousness for simply believing God. Second, we have the Mosaic Law, under which we have no chance of being justified or made righteous. These options are incompatible; we must take our pick.

This is why we cannot let the Law into the picture at all. Christ Jesus holds the promise of the covenant of salvation by grace. The Law of Moses doesn't even enter into this story! The inheritance of Jesus reaches directly back to the Abrahamic covenant.

The Jewish legalists—and subsequently the early Jewish Christians—assumed because God had given them the Law, following the Law was "the next step" in their ability to have a relationship with God. While they may have been experts in what the Mosaic Law (and subsequent additions to the Law) taught, they were not experts in the Abrahamic covenant, and as a result missed the big picture—the proper context for the Mosaic Law. They had missed the proverbial forest for the trees.

The Law is Good?

Paul, however, does not throw out the Law completely; he sees it as God-given and valuable. What he does say is that it cannot save us; it cannot impact our inheritance under the covenant. The teachers Paul is writing about had a high but distorted view of the Law. Paul also had a high view of the Law, but he understood it in its proper context, and knew it was a fatal mistake to hold such a view of the Law. When Paul asks in verse 19, "What, then, was the purpose of the law?" he knows this was the question on the Galatians' minds. He would probably be surprised to find this is still a question in many of our minds today, because we have had the benefit of his explanation for hundreds of years.

There are, by the way, several reasons for the law. Paul gives a couple of reasons to the Galatians, the first of which is found in verse 19, "It was added because of transgressions until the Seed to whom the promise referred had come." The Law made sin into transgressions (crimes). In other words, the Law took sin, which already existed, and made it a legal offense against God. Before the Law came, people saw and felt the effects of sin—and probably suffered from guilt as a result of it—but they did not know how terrible sin actually was. They couldn't know, until the Law was given that defined sin and expressed specific punishments for specific sins. The Law served as a wake-up call, a reality check.

Then, Paul writes (verses 21-23):

> Is the law, therefore, opposed to the promises of God? Absolutely not! For if a law had been given that could impart life, then righteousness would certainly have come by the law. But the Scripture declares that the whole world is a prisoner of sin, so that what was promised, being given through faith in Jesus Christ, might be given to those who believe.
>
> Before this faith came, we were held prisoners by the law, locked up until faith should be revealed.

The Law, again, was given because of sin, which existed prior to the Law. It was added to make sin bind to us, to make the effects of sin manifest. The Law functions like a traffic ticket; we can violate the posted speed without punishment until we get a speeding ticket; the ticket binds our speeding "sin" to us, making us liable for punishment.

Sin makes us a slave (John 8:34), and the Law lets us know we are slaves. It reveals how dire our situation is, and actually accentuates our sin problem. Before the Law, we could have shrugged sin off; but not since the Law was given. In other words, sin was the iron ball, and the Law was the chain that bound it to our ankles.

Everybody wants to get free from this bondage of sin, along with the associated feelings of guilt and anxiety. Some people try to avoid sin by saying that morality is relative, or they may blame genetics or evolution, and completely deny the existence of God. They know the effects of the Law, but they undermine it because they no longer want to feel guilty. Removing the Law may help shrug off guilt feelings, but it cannot help shrug off sin (Rom. 2:12-15). Remember, sin exists regardless of whether or not there is a law; the Law only addresses the legal ramifications of sin. The Law is not the problem; sin is the problem. Unfortunately, the Law is not the solution either. There is, however, another solution, and this is what the Good News is about.

The Law would work wonderfully if we were good by nature; however, because we are not, it condemns us. The Law, again, is not bad; it is us who are "bad." However, the Law does not give us salvation. The Law cannot give us life and it cannot give us right standing before God. Keeping the Law will not justify us, and doing away with the Law will not save us. The purpose of the Law is not to save us, or help us become closer to God; what the Law does is show us our need for a savior.

Recall in verse 1 of Galatians 3, Paul refers to this belief that we must add a little law to grace in order to maintain our right standing before God, suggesting that for the Galatians to have fallen for such a lie, someone had to have bewitched them. To Paul, any thinking that the Law is beneficial to our relationship with God is irrational and self-destructive; it must be witchcraft. This of course is a standard trick of our enemy; Satan is always trying to trick us into proving our goodness by keeping the Law. However, God gave us the Law, as Paul is pointing out, to prove we were sinners. Satan does not really care if we keep the Law and fall into pride and boasting, or fail miserably and feel guilty and defeated. He really does not care which we do; he has us either way.

A Second Reason for the Law

In verses 23-25, Paul now reveals a second reason for the Law:

> Before this faith came, we were held prisoners by the law, locked up until faith should be revealed. So the law was put in charge to lead us to Christ that we might be justified by faith. Now that faith has come, we are no longer under the supervision of the law.

In verse 24, the NIV reads, "the law was put in charge." Other translations say the Law was our custodian, or tutor. The picture we have from the Greek is that the Law was a temporary restraint and remedial teacher until faith could be revealed; this was its purpose in the history of Israel. The Law served to train and restrain Israel, to provide some spiritual and moral guidelines, until Jesus came.

The Greek word for "take charge of" is *pedagogue*. A pedagogue was a slave of a wealthy family who took responsibility for the children's education up until the time the children were of age. Wealthy families did not send their children to school; they hired or bought an educated slave who had complete control of the children's education in subjects like math and geography, as well as in the social mores of the culture, until the child became of age; at that point, the children were free of the pedagogue's authority and influence.

Therefore, when Paul refers to the Law as a pedagogue, he is saying a couple of important things which may not be obvious upon a casual reading. First, he is saying the Law was a slave—a lowly servant with the specific purpose of teaching the rudiments of knowledge and morality. Second, the Law as a pedagogue was a temporary employee. When Israel became "of age"—when the time for the Messiah had come—the Law's job was over; the position of tutor was no longer necessary.

Now that we are justified by faith in Jesus, we are no longer under the supervision of the Law. We are, as it were, "of age." The Law served its purpose, and its purpose is now over; the Law has been removed from service. We no longer have to answer to the demands of this pedagogue, nor can we. The Law's term is over and our pedagogue no longer has the authority to instruct us. As Paul says elsewhere, the Law has been completed, cancelled, nailed to the cross. At this point, we have to take an assessment of our education: Either the Law has done its job, or it has not. Either we have recognized our sin, or we have not. Either we have learned our need for a savior or we have not. This is it; we have had our chance. Continuing to follow the law will not lead us to faith, but into a bewitched state of delusion where we fall into either pride or despair. As Paul says in 2 Corinthians 3:6, the written code kills, but the Spirit gives life. Now that faith has come, the only means to the Christian life is through freedom in the Spirit.

CHAPTER 12: LIFE IN CHRIST

The impression most people have about grace and the Law is that they are opposed to one another. We say we are under grace so we are no longer under the Law, and to many this implies that one is good and the other is bad. Paul himself seems a little too negative about the Law at times; too hostile to the notion that there is any place for law in the Christian life. Then, he will say something that indicates this is not what he meant at all.

As we will see in a later chapter, when Paul describes Christian character, he does not talk in terms of keeping the Law, but he does describe a character that is law-abiding. The Holy Spirit is at work in us, producing character—the fruit of the Spirit—which by nature fulfills the law; as Paul writes in Romans 13:10, "… love is the fulfillment of the Law."

Living a law-abiding life is one of the effects of becoming a Christian; it is not, however, a *cause* of either becoming a Christian or holiness. Being law-abiding is a result of walking by the Spirit; it is not a qualification to *get* the Spirit. The Law, as we saw in the previous chapter, had other purposes: To demonstrate that sin was so serious an issue that the penalty for sin was death, and to show the absolute inability of human beings to keep it.

Keep this in mind about the Law: the Mosaic Law was so good, it became what is now known as the Judeo-Christian ethic, the basis for most civilized governments today, or at least those influenced by the Western world. The Law was an incredible gift to the entire world. We would not have anything remotely resembling what we consider civilization today if it were not for the Law that God gave to the Israelites.

Paul understood and appreciated the goodness of the Law, and did not consider the Law to be in competition with grace. They are not in competition—opposed to one another—because they belong in different categories. They have different purposes. The Law, in a sense, makes grace necessary. Conversely, the Law was necessary to show people to grace. The problem is when people confuse the two purposes, and look to the Law to make them righteous. However, the Law can only make you a sinner.

Paul's argument is we cannot become or remain righteous by keeping the Law because first, it is impossible. It was designed to reflect God's holiness, and man cannot possibly live up to that standard by human effort. Second, we undermine grace to even try to keep the Law. We are not supposed to keep the Law; we are supposed to realize "this is impossible," and turn to grace. Paul understood the separate and distinct functions of the Law and of grace, and wanted to make sure the Galatians—and others reading the letter—understood this as well. This principle was key to Martin Luther's theology, which could be summarized as "Law and Gospel." It is the Law that condemns us, and the Gospel of grace, which saves us. Without the law, we do not know that we need the Gospel. Without the Gospel, we cannot be saved, only condemned.

Three Characteristics of Life in Christ

The Christian life is intended to be lived in freedom; that is, not in bondage and not in fear. As Paul declares in Galatians 5:1, "It is for freedom that Christ has set us free." In Galatians 3:26-29, Paul gives the characteristics of this life of freedom in Christ:

> You are all sons of God through faith in Christ Jesus, for all of you who were baptized into Christ have clothed yourselves with Christ. There is neither Jew nor Greek, slave nor free, male nor female, for you are all one in Christ Jesus. If you belong to Christ, then you are Abraham's seed, and heirs according to the promise.

In these few verses, Paul states three positive effects deriving from being delivered from the supervision of the Law into the freedom of faith in Christ and the power of the Spirit: First, we become sons and daughters of God, with all the blessings coming from having God as Father. Second, we become related to each other on an equal basis; there is no longer age, rank, nationality, color, or sex separating us. All the things that could have separated us in the past—made some of us "in" and others "out"—have been removed in Christ. We are now one big family, each of us with equal rights. Third, we are now connected to God's history in Israel; we are Abraham's rightful heirs, and the Jewish history has become our history. We can read the Old Testament and say, "These are my ancestors; this is *my* story."

Relationship with God

In Christ, we are made sons and daughters of Almighty God. You may have heard the phrase at some point, "The family of God and the brotherhood of man," implying that God is the father of all people, and consequently we are all brothers and sisters. The Bible, however, does not teach anything of the kind. God is *not* everyone's father, and we are not all brothers and sisters. We are only related through Christ.

The Bible teaches that God is the father of one man; it does not talk about us being independently related to God as father. This one man, of course, is Jesus Christ. The only way we can become sons and daughters of God is by believing in Jesus. As John writes, "Yet to all who received him, to those who believed in his name, he gave the right to become children of God—children born not of natural descent, nor of human decision or a husband's will, but born of God" (John 1:12,13).

Furthermore, Paul wrote in Ephesians 1:4-5, "For he chose us in him before the creation of the world to be holy and blameless in his sight. In love he predestined us to be adopted as his sons through Jesus Christ…" Those of us who have been saved were chosen to be adopted. We aren't sons and daughters of God because He made us in His image; that just makes us his creation. We are children of God only because we are in Christ. Being a son or a daughter of God necessarily implies an intimacy not found in any other religion.

To be a son or a daughter of God means that we can, without inhibition, partake of everything He has; yet many, if not most of us, do not feel this freedom. We may know in our heads we are a son or daughter, but time and time again we find ourselves not feeling or acting like it. Often we tend to feel as if we are sneaking into the kitchen to grab a few scraps, never feeling the freedom to take everything we need or desire. And, should we take something from God, we often feel like we have to do something to pay Him back. Even though we may know the truth intellectually, deep down we do not really believe we deserve to receive anything from God.

This, however, is the entire point of grace—we do not deserve anything! However, grace is given to us freely anyway. Like many of you, I love to give things to my children, just to give to them. Even if they don't need anything, I give them gifts because it gives me joy. It's the nature of being a father. Jesus taught that God, being a perfect father, loves His children, and He loves to give to them.

Listen to the way you pray, to see how you view your relationship to the Father. Do you realize that more than ninety percent of the prayers in the New Testament are asking God for something? Many of us who have grown up in the church have been taught that prayer is a spiritual discipline and helps us grow spiritually; it's a duty, something we need to do as Christians. We've been taught how God loves to meet with us, He makes and appointment with us at six in the morning, and how dare we stand Him up—all kinds of weird, legalistic stuff. It just wrecks prayer.

Prayer is simply kids asking their dad for stuff; asking God for what you need or you want. Look at the Lord's Prayer: "Give us this day our daily bread…" *Give.* "Lead us not into temptation, but deliver us from the evil one." It is all asking—for things we either want or need.

Even if we consider that God is not just our Father but also God, we *still*, through Jesus, have the right to approach Him whenever we want. Consider what the writer of Hebrews says in Chapter 4:14-16:

> Therefore, since we have a great high priest who has gone through the heavens, Jesus the Son of God, let us hold firmly to the faith we profess. For we do not have a high priest who is unable to sympathize with our weaknesses, but we have one who has been tempted in every way, just as we are—yet was without sin. Let us then approach the throne of grace with confidence, so that we may receive mercy and find grace to help us in our time of need.

The King James Version even says, "Let us therefore come *boldly*..." We are free, in Christ, to approach God as Father, as Creator, or as King.

One in Christ

The freedom we have in Christ is first and foremost freedom with God; however, we have also been given freedom toward each other. No longer is there any Greek or Jew; or, to put it in a more current context, no longer any black, white, Hispanic, Asian, Arab, Native American or Jew. There is no master or servant, employer or employee. Each of us is entitled in Christ to relate to any other Christian on equal terms, whether he's the church janitor or the Pope.

Obviously, this does not mean these adjectives and roles no longer exist. I will be a white Anglo-Saxon male for the rest of my earthly life. I am a husband and father, and have responsibilities accordingly. There are also employers and employees (who sometimes may feel like slaves), and these roles will continue to exist. There will remain those who are rich and those who are poor. In the church, there will remain the necessity of functional leadership and there will be people to be led. Paul is not in any sense suggesting there should be anarchy.

What Paul means is that before God all have equal footing, no matter what their positions are on Earth. God's grace is poured out equally on all flesh. The Holy Spirit is given to all, without regard to race, sex, or tax bracket, as are the gifts of the Spirit; which means, of course, that even the youngest and most immature members of the church can exercise prophetic gifts and heal the sick. This doesn't mean he should be the pastor, but it does mean God values all people equally and can use anyone He wishes. Therefore, we should not devalue anyone.

Of course, Paul is speaking here specifically about the division between Jews (the chosen people) and Gentiles (the non-chosen people). If we are not of Jewish descent, we are Gentiles; or rather, *were* Gentiles. This dividing line has now been erased, and anyone—even uncircumcised Gentile "dogs"—can become a descendant of Abraham through faith. All of us who are in Christ are a part of God's big family. We are adopted sons and daughters of God, and therefore related to each other. Furthermore, we are sons and daughters of Abraham, heirs of the Covenant promise. Israel's history is now our history; our family tree is rooted firmly in Abraham.

So, What's Not to Like?

In light of what we have been freely given in Christ, Paul now asks, "Why would you give all this up?" Let's look at Galatians 4:8-11:

> Formerly, when you did not know God, you were slaves to those who by nature are not gods. But now that you know God—or rather are known by God—how is it that you are turning back to those weak and miserable principles? Do you wish to be enslaved by them all over again? You are observing special days and months and seasons and years! I fear for you, that somehow I have wasted my efforts on you.

The Galatians knew the bondage from which they had been freed; they had left lives of slavery to be adopted into God's family where they were neither slaves nor servants. In Christ, they had been set free and handed an inheritance. According to Paul, a "Christian" form of legalism is no better than idolatry!

All we have been given is forfeited when we exchange a simple faith in Christ for a life of religious performance. All of the blessings of Life—the blessings that we gain through relationship with Jesus—

are lost to us if we give in to legalism. As we have seen in the past, Paul is very clear on this point: it is Jesus plus nothing. Any attempts to add to what Christ has done, no matter how good it may seem, disqualify us from *all* of God's blessings.

Before we trusted in Christ, we were slaves. We were slaves to sin, slaves to the law, and slaves to the demonic entities that attach themselves to God's laws and condemn us. Satan has taken the law, which was meant to serve as our schoolmaster, and turned it into a bludgeon with which to condemn us. The Galatians—who had been slaves, not to the Law, but to sin—had been set free by the Gospel which Paul had preached. How did Paul say they are once again becoming enslaved? By simply trying to earn what they have already received for free, thereby moving from one form of slavery to another.

Trying to earn holiness—for it is indeed holiness we have been given—by keeping special days, fasting, tithing, quiet times and Bible reading is not only a waste of time, it is actually counter-productive! For, by trying to earn holiness, we actually lose it. In trying to "become" holy, we become enslaved to the law and the sin from which we were already set free. Now don't misunderstand me—I am not saying that things like tithing and quiet times are not good. What I am saying, and what Paul is saying, is if we think these things make us more holy, we are dead wrong. We are holy only because of Jesus. We read the Bible, pray and tithe not to become holy, but *because we can*.

Because of Jesus, we have been made as holy—which in essence means to be set apart for God—as we could ever hope to be. *We cannot be made any more holy*! And, if we try to get "more holy" by being religious or what we consider to be "spiritual," we don't get more holy, we get <u>un</u>holy. By trying to achieve a higher state of holiness, we unplug from God to plug into our own work.

This does not mean, however, that we instantly become Christlike. Certainly, this is not the case, and no one is suggesting that we become morally pure upon our initial salvation. Legally, yes. Practically, no. However, from the moment we receive the Holy Spirit, the Spirit begins to work in us, transforming us into Christ's image. As Paul wrote in 2 Cor. 3:17,18:

> Now the Lord is the Spirit, and where the Spirit of the Lord is, there is freedom. And we, who with unveiled faces all reflect the Lord's glory, are being transformed into his likeness with ever-increasing glory, which comes from the Lord, who is the Spirit.

We, in freedom, are being transformed into the likeness of Christ by grace—the powerful presence of the Holy Spirit. We do not become holy or holier by jumping through religious hoops or by doing good works. This is why Paul wonders if he has wasted his time bringing the Gospel to the Galatians (v 4:11). I do not think he is merely being dramatic; Paul is being very, very serious. Notice Paul is not saying, "Well, at least they've got *some* truth." Contrast this with Philippians 1:18, where he says, "It doesn't matter. In any event, whether for the right or the wrong reasons, Christ is being preached." No, if the Galatians continue to choose a life of religiosity, Paul says the Gospel has been lost.

Holidays are Bad, Too?

Notice something else in this passage: Up to this point, Paul had been specifically addressing the issue of circumcision. Here, he mentions another form of legalism, which he seems to consider equally evil:

> You are observing special days and months and seasons and years! I fear for you, that somehow I have wasted my efforts on you. (Gal. 4:10,11)

Some people have tried to make the case that Paul was referring to the pagan holidays that the Galatians had observed prior to converting to Christianity. Certainly, this was an issue for the Galatians; these pagan celebrations were part of their culture, and part of their civic calendar as well. A decision to not observe them created an issue with their family, friends and culture. A modern example would be a Muslim converting to Christianity; they would immediately stop celebrating Islamic holidays, which would create major problems in a predominantly Muslim community. However, I don't think we can conclude that this is what Paul was talking about.

The context of Paul's letter to the Galatians has nothing to do with reverting to paganism; the issue was the influence of Jewish Christians who were leading the Galatian church into a mix of Judaism and Christianity. The Jewish Christians had an issue with Gentiles being saved but not having to pay attention to the Jewish traditions. It is only logical that besides circumcision, they also taught that keeping the Jewish calendar was necessary for Christians to maintain their righteousness.

Furthermore, had the Galatians fallen back into keeping pagan holidays, these Jewish Christians no doubt would have put a stop to it; it is not logical that these Jews would have come preaching circumcision and the Law and still allowed this idolatry. I think we have to conclude that Paul was specifically talking about the Galatians' observance of the Jewish holy days.

So, does this mean we can no longer celebrate Christmas? I don't think so; remember, "It is for freedom that Christ has set us free." There is a difference between choosing to celebrate at certain times of the year and believing that we *must* observe certain days to maintain our holiness. I do think that some Christians' beliefs about keeping the Sabbath, for example, fall into the category of legalism, especially those who insist Saturday is the only proper day to worship. Going to church on Saturday (or Sunday) doesn't make you more holy and missing church altogether doesn't make you any less holy—although there are many, many good reasons for regular church attendance and fellowship. Keeping the Sabbath is a good thing; however, it doesn't make you any more righteous than someone who works on Sunday. Paul addressed this issue in Romans 14:5,6:

> One man considers one day more sacred than another; another man considers every day alike. Each one should be fully convinced in his own mind. He who regards one day as special, does so to the Lord. He who eats meat, eats to the Lord, for he gives thanks to God; and he who abstains, does so to the Lord and gives thanks to God.

Many of us continue to do these religious things for religious reasons even though in our heads we know the truth. The problem is, we don't feel worthy of either salvation or our freedom, and are compelled by our human nature to try to do things to become worthy. What we have to believe and pray into our hearts is the truth that *of course* we're not worthy—once again, this is precisely the point. This is what the Law tells us; this is the point of grace. If we were worthy, we wouldn't need grace.

You have probably heard the platitude, "Let go and let God." As trite as this seems, with regard to our righteousness this concept is crucial. Let go of the need to become worthy, because it will never happen. Let go of the need to become more holy, because this, too, is impossible (more Christlike, yes—but again, that is the Holy Spirit's work). Let these needs go and let God bless you with all the good things He has already given freely to you—then you will actually begin to discover that the Spirit working in you is conforming you more and more to the image of Christ.

CHAPTER 13: WHAT IT MEANS TO BE FREE

> It is for freedom that Christ has set us free. Stand firm, then, and do not let yourselves be burdened again by a yoke of slavery. Mark my words! I, Paul, tell you that if you let yourselves be circumcised, Christ will be of no value to you at all. Again I declare to every man who lets himself be circumcised that he is obligated to obey the whole law. You who are trying to be justified by law have been alienated from Christ; you have fallen away from grace. But by faith we eagerly await through the Spirit the righteousness for which we hope. For in Christ Jesus neither circumcision nor uncircumcision has any value. The only thing that counts is faith expressing itself through love. (Gal. 5:1-6)

"It is for freedom that Christ has set us free." It is difficult for me to imagine a more radical definition of authentic humanity. According to Paul, God's purpose in making us free is not so we can fulfill the great commission, feed the hungry, or become martyrs. God's primary purpose in making us free is simply to be free and remain free. Christ made us free for *freedom*. Freedom, according to Paul, is an end in itself. Jesus has made us free so we could be authentically who we are, and become who we were destined to be.

Considering what many of us have heard preached (or have preached ourselves!), we would get the impression we have not been saved to be free; rather, we have been saved—set free from the bondage of sin—to become in bondage to religious expectations. The contrast seems to be between the bondage to Satan on one hand, and bondage to God on the other. However, consider this: *The devil doesn't care what we are in bondage to, as long as we are in bondage*! The devil is not committed to a morality (or immorality); he is merely committed to keeping us away from Christ! And you know what? Religion works better than anything else possibly could.

When someone is enslaved in sin, they know they're miserable. They know they aren't following God and when the Gospel is presented, at least they can tell the difference between the Gospel and whatever they are in bondage to. There is hope for these people; in some ways, they are perhaps closer to the Kingdom of God than those stuck in religion. However, when you are enslaved by religion, you're in real trouble. When you are a "good" person—keeping whatever rules are laid out for you and thinking like the Pharisees that this obedience is making you holier than you were before—you often can't tell the difference between freedom and bondage.

People who are in bondage to religion read the Bible, pray, fast, and do good works. What do people saved by grace do? They read the Bible, fast, pray, and do good works (whoa… *déjà vu*!). The difference is that some people are doing these things in bondage and are not getting anywhere, except deeper in bondage. The people under grace are getting freer, more empowered, and full of life. You see, religion still keeps you away from Christ, but you can't recognize your predicament. If you come out of the gutter into religion, it is really no net loss to Satan; for him it's merely a personnel issue: in effect, he just assigns you different demons.

When we were saved, many of us were told to stop doing the things on list "A" and to start doing the things on list "B." Now, there is nothing wrong with changing your behavior; in fact, this is a by-product of grace. When we receive the Holy Spirit, we begin to desire to do good works instead of bad works. However, for many Christian leaders the priority is not the freedom to grow, but sin management. In fact, "freedom" is a very scary word for many pastors. Keeping people free is often the last thing on their mind, as they are so focused on keeping their people from sinning (or what they *perceive* is sinning). However, freedom is the first priority for Paul. We were made free to be free.

The Westminster Confession states, "Man's chief end is to glorify God, and to enjoy him forever." That's not a bad answer; however, I would have to say that according to Galatians 5:1, the chief end of man is to get free and to stay free. Christ died to make us free. If Christ didn't intend for us to be free, why set us free in the first place?

The Jews had a pretty great religion happening already. Jesus could have just given us the Sermon on the Mount and let it go at that, but He didn't. No, his teachings were not enough; the Jews did not need another rabbinic teaching. Jesus' intent was not to teach people to freedom; rather, his teachings proved there was no hope in trying to work for our salvation. He died and rose again to make us free—so we wouldn't have to work for our freedom.

Man was created in God's image. If we look at what was intended for Adam and Eve in Eden, we can see that freedom is mankind's native environment. Man put himself in bondage by trying to achieve something on his own when he ate the apple rather than relying on God for knowledge. Eating the apple was in effect man's first attempt at religion—his first attempt at self-righteousness. "Eat the apple, and you will be like God" is the same lie as any holiness doctrine.

The Difference between Holiness and Being Holy

Each of Paul's letters is divided into two sections, the *indicative* and the *imperative.* He begins by telling us who we are in Christ, the indicative. Then, after he has set this foundation of our identity and reveals the blessings we have in Christ, he progresses to the imperative, telling us "in light of who you are, this is how you ought to act." No matter how much we talk about grace and freedom, and how we can't gain relationship with God through our performance, we cannot make the mistake of thinking that how we behave isn't important. Paul never gives the impression he doesn't care how we act. In fact, the imperative sections of his letters are so strong that they are often interpreted as "New Testament Laws," which form the basis for much of Christian legalism.

However, Paul is not giving us new laws to follow, nor is he advocating licentiousness. What Paul is saying is, "Because of who we are, because we are free, this is how our lives should look." It is for freedom that Christ has set us free, therefore, Paul says to stand firm in freedom and do not become enslaved again (either in sin or in religion). He puts the responsibility for our staying free squarely on us.

We can't merely acknowledge that Christ has made us free and then think our freedom is guaranteed; we simply don't live in that kind of a world. We live in a world where anyone who has any kind of freedom at all will have powerful forces attempting to enslave them again. This is true in the spiritual world, as well the physical. We have been given freedom in Christ, and now there are going to be demonic forces, religious forces, social forces, as well as your own internal personality forces that will try to undermine that freedom and seek to enslave you all over again. You are going to have to fight to protect your own freedom.

The forces of bondage and enslavement are in the air we breathe, at every level, in every culture in the world. These forces are at work in any bureaucracy (just pay attention to the news for a few days), and to some extent they are at work in every church. This is the reason we have to constantly fight to maintain our freedom from these forces seeking to bring us back into bondage.

Around the world there is a kind of spontaneous liberation movement happening, where totalitarianism is being replaced with various forms of democracy. However, in countries where freedom is now taken for granted, the trend is the opposite: Over the past one hundred or so years we have been steadily losing the freedoms fought for by our founding fathers. The sheer number of rules and regulations is growing at an alarming rate.

Bureaucracies are inherently enslaving; that is simply the reality of the fallen world we live in. Like everything else, any system created by man is defective, and there are natural as well as supernatural forces waiting to take advantage of those deficiencies. We are not born free; as in the movie *The Matrix*, we are born slaves in a fallen world that wants to keep us enslaved. Jesus died to make us free, and we have got to continue to fight in order to stay free; you cannot afford to be passive about your freedom. If you don't fight, I can guarantee you are going to come into bondage.

This is true at every level—and those forces you see out there in the world are also at work in your heart and in the church. Both in the world and in the church, there is a general tendency for people to want to be taken care of. They want their decision-making responsibilities taken away from them, and these forces of evil are more than willing to step in and take over those roles. However, whether they are social or demonic, these forces are no match for the Holy Spirit who lives inside of us. He who is in us is stronger than he who is in the world. We really have nothing to fear from evil spirits or anything else; they are no match for the power of God at work in our lives.

The Fear of Freedom

I suspect the main reason most people give up their freedoms is their own personality flaws. Freedom is terrifying; it produces a lot of anxiety in many people. On my twenty-first birthday, I [Ken] received a draft notice. I was upset about this, as on one hand it represented a significant loss of freedom, not to mention the potential danger of the Vietnam War. But at the same time, I felt this perverse sense of peace and comfort when I thought, "At least someone else will take responsibility for my life for the next couple of years." Bondage can be comforting, as freedom (or its corresponding responsibility) can be downright terrifying.

Christians create religious systems for exactly this reason. Freedom on a day-to-day basis (living by the Spirit) is too much work, involves too much responsibility, and is too terrifying—so, people invent rules against dancing, or jewelry, or any number of things. There is safety in boundaries. Once these rules have been made, the responsibility of making decisions is gone. You are now in bondage to your rules, but you no longer have to think. This apparently works, because I've met many people who have told me amazing stories of spiritual abuse, but yet they keep going back to be enslaved once again. Why else would they do this, if not for the fact that they prefer bondage to freedom?

There are also people who look for a "word from God" for everything they do. They fast, they pray, they cry, and they seek after prophets, but they never seem to hear what they need to hear. Do you know why they don't hear from God? It's because God has already given us all things pertaining to life and godliness (2 Peter 1:3). In other words, "I have made you free; now go and make your own decisions." God does not tell us everything, and He certainly won't decide everything for us. He does give wisdom to all who ask; however, this doesn't mean He gives us all of the specifics—in fact, if God told us every little thing to do, why would He need to give us wisdom? At times He will give specific direction; other times, however, He wants us to make decisions on our own, out of what He's already given us. It's part of our growth, working out who we are, as being created in God's image.

The people who do claim to hear from God about all of their decisions—who are so afraid of making wrong choices that they make God the responsible person—typically make the worst decisions of anyone I know. These are not bad people; they are good, and quite sincere. They just don't want the responsibility of making their own choices and taking responsibility for themselves. So, they say things like "God told me to buy that car." Then, when things go wrong, they claim it was God's will and dream up some spiritual reasoning about some lesson God wanted to teach them. Freedom and the responsibility of making mistakes are terrifying to many people.

Christ has set us free from bondage and from fear. The good news is, whether we make good choices or bad, God loves us. You see, God is in the *redemption* business. He doesn't pull strings or force obedience. Instead, He redeems our choices. If we make good choices, he still needs to redeem us. Know this: You've never made a perfectly good choice in your life! Every choice you have made is tainted with some kind of selfishness or brokenness or just plain stupidity. All we can do is make the best decisions possible with the circumstances we have, and know that God will turn it into good. We need to be forgiven, not only for our failures, but also for our successes, because they are all short of perfection.

God deals with broken people in a broken world; he redeems and heals everything we do. This is why we have been made free; it's so we can exercise our freedom. You can defend your freedom to make decisions, because God works all things—the good things and the bad—together for the good of those who love him (Rom. 8:28). God is with you. God is there redeeming your decisions, not because you are good or bad, but because you are His child.

The Blame Game

Another way people avoid responsibility for their decisions is by blaming others. We have already seen an example with some people's inclination to blame God ("God told me ..."). God, of course, is an "all purpose" person to assign blame to, as we can give him the responsibility for things that work out ("I'd like to thank God for this Grammy...") and for things that don't ("God told me to marry him, it must have been for a reason," or one that really bugs me, "God gave me this illness for a reason.").

While some Christians will, during a crisis of faith, blame God for some of the bad things in their lives, many are more comfortable blaming Satan for anything bad, from sickness to flat tires to oversleeping. I don't doubt that such a thing as spiritual warfare exists; in fact, I'm positive it does. However, if you smoke for twenty years, don't blame your bad lungs on the devil.

With the advent of psychology and modern counseling methods, it has also become popular to blame other people for our failures. For example, you might say your father abused you, and therefore you are messed up. And you might actually be right—there is no doubt that childhood scars have a significant impact on who we become. But, here's the thing: If you are in Christ and he has made you free, you can no longer blame your father or anyone else for the decisions you make today. If Christ has set you free, you *are* free indeed. You are free to make choices—you can respond to people any way you want—regardless of how you were injured as a child. If you stay messed up, it's *your* choice, not your father's.

A common excuse for adultery is to shift blame to their spouse for no longer being interested in them, or to say he or she doesn't understand them anymore. So what? You might be right, and your spouse may be sinning in their attitude toward you. However, you are free—you make your choices, whatever they will be. No one else has made your decision for you.

Real freedom is scary, because real freedom means real choices and real responsibility. If you are free, your life is not going to look like social forces, or life chances, but your life will look like *your* choices. This really is a scary thing, unless we forget God's redemptive power; God doesn't necessarily *fix* the things we mess up, but He does redeem them, working everything for good.

We have no more excuses, not because we're under judgment, but because we are free. We all have various reasons for things being the way they are; however, if we are truly free, then we can no longer blame anything in our past. It's all rooted in the Gospel; it's all under the forgiving blood of Christ. In the end, your life will look like your choices, but you won't be condemned for the way your life looks. It's all forgiven, and all will be redeemed.

One of the biggest decisions that people will ever make is who they will marry, and it is not uncommon for people to wonder, "Is he or she *the One*?" Some people worry themselves sick over this, especially in the first year of marriage if things get a bit rocky. Let's not even talk about whether there actually is "the one" for each of us. In reality, it doesn't matter. What if we make a wrong choice? Don't you think God is powerful enough to redeem that bad decision and turn him or her *into* "the one?"

There are really two questions at issue here. "Do you *believe* God can redeem your choices?" and, "Do you believe God *will* redeem your choices?" The first question goes right to the heart of our being responsible to make our own choices. The second is simply a matter of our faith.

To have Christ is to have freedom. As John said, "you will know the Truth (Jesus) and the Truth will set you free" (John 8:32). When you know Jesus, you have freedom in action. When you do not have freedom of choice—when you do things because of rules or social pressure or religion—then you are not free, and you don't have Christ.

Paul is Still Angry

In Galatians 5 verses 7-12, we can see Paul continuing to express his outrage at those who have thrown the Galatians into confusion:

> You were running a good race. Who cut in on you and kept you from obeying the truth? That kind of persuasion does not come from the one who calls you. "A little yeast works through the whole batch of dough." I am confident in the Lord that you will take no other view. The one who is throwing you into confusion will pay the penalty, whoever he may be. Brothers, if I am still preaching circumcision, why am I still being persecuted? In that case the offense of the cross has been abolished. As for those agitators, I wish they would go the whole way and emasculate themselves!

Paul still cannot believe that the Galatians can be so stupid as to trade freedom for bondage, even though he acknowledges someone has "cut in" and confused them. There is a good chance Paul is referring to the spiritual powers behind religious bondage, but he is also referring to those men who perpetrate these lies.

See again how serious an issue this is for Paul; he repeats, in even stronger terms, that to preach circumcision is to abolish the offense of the cross! Not only would Paul have been wasting his time, but Jesus' death would have been a waste of time! Therefore, he wishes those preaching circumcision and a continued life of religious observance would go ahead and castrate themselves. This isn't the kind of nice, encouraging talk you normally hear in church.

Soft on Sin?

Paul is angry and insistent that you either have Christ, or you have bondage. It's either one or the other. Paul's insistence about following laws putting us into bondage led to the accusation that Paul was soft on sin, of encouraging lawlessness. We've seen that this was not the case; however his focus on freedom struck the religious people as being heretical, and they accused him of promoting sin. But listen to this: if you aren't accused by the religious of being soft on sin, if you aren't accused of encouraging people to be "too free," then you are not yet preaching the Gospel.

But Paul, who did preach the gospel, heard these accusations and perhaps this is why he responds thusly in verse 13-15:

> You, my brothers, were called to be free. But do not use your freedom to indulge the sinful nature; rather, serve one another in love. The entire law is summed up in a single command: "Love your neighbor as yourself." If you keep on biting and devouring each other, watch out or you will be destroyed by each other.

Paul isn't teaching that we now have freedom to sin. In fact, there is no such thing as freedom to sin. Sin by definition is bondage; the measure in which we sin is the measure of our bondage to sin. If we choose sin, we have left freedom behind. Remember, it is not for bondage that we have been set free; it is for freedom that we have been set free. We are not "free" to sin; we are free *not* to sin.

Free To Love

This is how Paul defines true freedom: True freedom is not freedom to indulge our sinful nature; true freedom is when we are free to serve one another out of love. The ultimate test of freedom is being able to serve each other, not because we have to, but because we want to. Because we ourselves have been accepted freely, we can accept others freely.

Being in bondage means we need to worry about our own acceptance, and as a result we are not free to accept each other as we should. Being in bondage means we are not free to give love away; it means living lives of selfishness. But being free means we are free from own selfishness and fear. We don't have to try to work for anything, it's all a gift. We have so much, in fact, that we can freely give to others, even if they have nothing to give back to us. This is Paul's definition of true freedom. We are now free to serve God and each other.

When we can love each other unconditionally, even when we are not loved back, when we can give freely to those who don't deserve it; when we serve others not because we are told to, but because we want to, then we know we are free indeed.

CHAPTER 14: UNDERSTANDING INTERNAL CONFLICT

Every Christian alive feels from time to time as if he or she is a walking civil war. You have the old fallen nature tugging at your new redeemed nature, and this creates conflict and pain, and often leads to feelings of shame and depression. By "walking civil war," I am referring to the ongoing struggle between what we know we ought to be and what are. Paul refers to this as the struggle between the spirit and the sinful nature ("flesh" in some translations), and now gives the Galatians the key to winning that war:

> So I say, live by the Spirit, and you will not gratify the desires of the sinful nature. For the sinful nature desires what is contrary to the Spirit, and the Spirit what is contrary to the sinful nature. They are in conflict with each other, so that you do not do what you want. But if you are led by the Spirit, you are not under law. (Gal. 5:16-18)

Paul then goes on to list some traits of the sinful nature and contrasts these things with the fruit of the Spirit that many of us learned in Sunday School: love, joy, peace, patience, kindness, goodness, faithfulness, gentleness, and self-control. Paul cleverly points out that even if the Law was still in effect, there are no laws against any of this spiritual fruit. An acquaintance of mine [Alden] once complained about all of the traffic cops sitting at speed traps around our town, needing to catch their monthly quota of speeders. I replied, "I have a great plan. I know how to totally frustrate them. This is what we do: We all drive within speed limit; then they won't be able to write any tickets." He looked at me like I was nuts, but I think he got the point—if you do good things, you won't have to worry about the laws. The fruit of the Spirit will create in us the desire to do good things; we no longer will be looking for ways around the laws, we will simply be looking for good things to do.

In verse 24, Paul says something quite interesting about our old, sinful nature: "Those who belong to Christ Jesus have crucified the sinful nature with its passions and desires." Paul states clearly here that our sinful nature has been crucified. "Have (or has) crucified," if you will notice, is past tense. Our sinful nature has been killed, it is now dead, and it is over and done with. In Romans 6:6, Paul writes, "For we know that our old self *was crucified* with him so that the body of sin might be done away with… (italics mine)." It's not your job to die to yourself, crucify the flesh, or whatever spiritual-sounding phrase you may have heard. And, not only is it not your job, it's already been accomplished in Jesus. You simply have no more sinful nature to crucify. Looking back a few pages, Paul has already made this point clear to the Galatians:

> I have been crucified with Christ and I no longer live, but Christ lives in me. The life I live in the body, I live by faith in the Son of God, who loved me and gave himself for me. (Gal. 2:20)

This is, granted, confusing. Objectively, your sinful nature has been crucified. It's dead; it no longer has any right to live. What looks like life is merely momentum from before the cross. I've heard hunters tell of grizzly bears that have been shot directly in the brain while charging, and yet they keep coming because of the residual energy in their nervous system. This is kind of how our sinful nature is. The sinful nature is dead; however, it still has a huge amount of inertia built up so it still goes on hurting and damaging. It's still real, you can still be hurt by it, but it really is dead.

In many Bible translations, as I have said, "sinful nature" is translated "flesh." The word "flesh," while including our body, does not only refer to physical flesh. Flesh is not sexual sin, drunkenness, and debauchery, although the concept does include these; they are mere footnotes to the larger picture of "flesh." The simple but comprehensive Biblical definition of flesh is this: It's seeing life from a human perspective and living life with human power. This definition is the key to understanding how to assess the spiritual struggle that we are in and how to overcome it.

Conversely, the simple, comprehensive, Biblical definition of "living by the Spirit" is not being "spiritual" or "mystical" or anything of this nature. Being spiritual in the Biblical sense is seeing life from God's point of view, and living life through God's power.

We were all born into the realm of the flesh. We were born into a mortal body which is limited; it is subject to sin, sickness, and it is destined to die. These are all characteristics of the flesh. Your mind is, likewise, flesh. It is limited; it is prone to sickness, sin, and entropy. We were born into a human, fleshly world with a human, fleshly worldview. This worldview is also limited and subject to sin. It operates in rebellion to God and it will pass away. Flesh, in all its aspects, is limited by human limitations and by human mortality.

Trying to live life and solve problems based on a defective human perspective is the reason the world is in the mess that it is, and the reason why the world will never work. Even if inspired by Biblical principles, human governments operate according to human perspectives. I am not saying that we shouldn't get involved in politics, but we need to be aware that the only way we will truly solve anything is by getting God's perspective and operating in Gods' power.

Don't put your hopes in low interest rates, the stock market, or a good health plan. Don't put your hopes in getting the right job, or in electing the right president. Put your hope in God, because He is the only person who can radically solve your problems and heal the world we live in. One of the roles of the Church in the world is to see more healing come to the world. It only comes through God's perspective and God's power, not by manipulating any world system.

Christians have been born twice—once into the common, human, flesh world, and "again" into a Spirit realm and gifted with a whole new set of possibilities. We are no longer limited by a human perspective. We have been given access to the Spirit—to God's perspective. Likewise we are no longer limited by mere human power, doomed to failure. We now have access to God's unlimited power.

Having God's perspective would only bring frustration if we were still limited to human power; thankfully, we also have God's power to effect change on the world. The rules have been changed. We have stepped through a doorway into a new dimension where the old limitations of the flesh and the old laws of entropy and death don't apply. In this new realm of the Spirit, there are no such limitations. With God, all things are possible. I can do all things through Christ who strengthens me.

In the Spirit, we have potential that is simply not available to those still trapped in the flesh. No matter how successful or gifted they seem, they do not have the resources or the potential that is available to the least in the Kingdom of God. Those who have not yet said "yes" to Christ are stuck with only one defective, human perspective and human source of power; those who have received the gift of the Holy Spirit have access to a whole new realm.

Therefore, the Christian now has the option to live either in the flesh, according to their human potential, or to live in the Spirit with all of the potential available in the Spirit. This is what is implied by Galatians 5:16-18. From now on, the quality of your life is largely determined by the choices you make, both in little things and in big things. You may either live according to the flesh or according to the Spirit. God, of course, redeems our mistakes; however, our choices still impact the immediate quality of our life on Earth.

God's Perspective

To understand God's perspective, we must begin with John 3:16—"God loved you so much that He gave His only son in exchange for you (my paraphrase)." That's how much you are loved. Many of us don't feel loved; however this does not change the fact that you are loved by God. To understand God's perspective we must accept this as fact, no matter how we feel. In 1 Corinthians 14, Paul writes that we are supernaturally gifted and empowered in ways which are humanly impossible. We might not feel supernaturally gifted—that, however, does not mean it isn't true.

If you have the Holy Spirit indwelling you, then you have within you a whole new set of options, along with the potential to make these options reality. You now can get free from sin and habits which have bound you all of your life. You can grow. You can pray and see the circumstances around you changed. This is how we look from God's perspective and as such, this is objective reality. Likewise, seeing life from God's perspective, we can know that we are forgiven (Hebrews 10:18), complete (Col. 2:10), redeemed (Col.

1:14), powerful (Romans 1:16), accepted (Romans 14:3), needed (1Cor. 12), and rich (1 Cor. 1:5). We are blessed with every spiritual blessing (Eph. 1:3), we have life (Romans 5:18), we are perfect (Hebrews 10:14)—and this is just a partial list! These things are all objectively true; that is, they are true whether or not we feel like they are true.

To live life in the Sprit, we must first accept God's perspective and then act accordingly. God's view of you must first be firmly in your mind. This, by the way, is one reason why we read the Bible. We don't read it to get spiritual points or to find new rules to follow. We read the Bible to save our lives! We read the Bible so we can first get God's perspective of who we are, to know what it means to live in the Spiritual realm. Life in the Sprit is so bizarre, so contrary to life in the flesh, that without the Holy Spirit and God's word, we could never get it! Many of us still don't, because we insist on reading the Bible "in the flesh"—from a human perspective. Read it, and let the Holy Spirit reveal God's perspective.

The War with the Flesh

The war with the flesh is in full force at this point. The flesh, along with the prodding of Satan, will come in counterattack. You read the Bible and discover truth. You find out you are okay with God. You find out you are loved, and that you have access to this amazing realm of the Spirit. The flesh will then come to give you its subjective, defective perspective: you aren't loved, you aren't okay with God, you are a sinner and you aren't powerful. You must work to be loved. You must try harder to be accepted.

You are now in the midst of this civil war, this "war of the worlds," so to speak. This is where you choose to believe Paul: "So I say, live by the Spirit and you will not gratify the sinful desires of the flesh." Living by the Spirit means believing the truth of the new spiritual realm and not the lies of the flesh. People will lie to you all of the time; you can't stop this. What you *can* do, however, is to stop believing the lies. If you know the truth, you can dismiss lies and choose to act according to the truth. The problem is that we feel obligated to act on these horrible thoughts that attack us—that we're not worthy, not gifted or not holy—because it seems right to our fallen human perspective. Either we give up, or we take the opposite approach and work harder.

The truth is that neither of these human approaches is appropriate. You only have to deal with these issues if you choose to live according to the flesh. But Paul gives us our battle plan: Believe the truth and act accordingly. This is not to say we won't still have feelings associated with the lies; they may be painful and may hurt us. But now knowing the truth, we can dismiss these lies and choose to live according to the truth of the Spirit.

The first step in fighting this battle is to say, "I don't feel worthy, but this feeling doesn't reflect God's truth. God's perspective is that He has made me worthy." Again, we've got to be firm in the truth of God's perspective. We may not feel it, but at the very least we need to know it mentally. The issue is never whether we believe, or whether we have faith. Belief is a matter of choice: The issue for us is always, "Who do we choose to believe? Where do we choose to place our faith?" This is what we need to choose to believe: "His divine power has given you everything you need for life and godliness through our knowledge of him who called us by his own glory and his own goodness" (2 Peter 1:3). You have been given everything you need for life and godliness, as a free gift. You have everything, in Jesus.

The reason Paul cares so much about this can be found in his letter to the Colossians:

> My purpose is that they may be encouraged in heart and united in love, so that they may have the full riches of

> complete understanding, in order that they may know the mystery of God, namely, Christ, in whom are hidden all the treasures of wisdom and knowledge. I tell you this so that no one may deceive you by fine-sounding arguments. (Col. 2:2-4)

Religion says to concentrate on your conduct, to concentrate on changing your behavior. According to some counseling theories, if we change someone's behavior, we can change their life. There is some truth to that, obviously, but only if we are choosing to live by the flesh. It's dangerous for Christians to fall into this trap, because it is indeed a trap; it keeps them operating in the flesh and preempts life in the Spirit. This approach—dubbed "sin management" by some unknown genius—has been in use by the church for hundreds of years, though it's obvious that it isn't Biblical, and it doesn't work!

The thinking is that if we can keep people from sinning, we can make them into good Christians (or at least they'll look good from the outside). God's perspective says, "No, you can't." Keeping people from sinning only makes them legalists! Getting people to read the Bible and go to prayer meetings won't make them good Christians; it just makes them Pharisees! Eventually they will turn into a common caricature of Christianity: guilt-ridden, beaten-down, and abused. We've got to be built up in the truth. We need to have a strong foundation of grace. Getting God's perspective is at least half of living according to the Spirit.

The Flesh Strikes Back

In dealing with this internal conflict, the "flesh" will attempt to trick us into reconciling the conflict in a couple of ways: First, the flesh will say, in effect, that what you choose to believe is reality. Just ignore your human reality, deny your feelings, and pretend things are true when they are not. This kind of thinking is nothing less than religious addiction: using religion, including worship, prayer and other religious activities and ideas to protect you from the real, painful world you live in. Religious addicts use religion in the same way other addicts use drugs, alcohol or sex: to deny their pain. They pretend that religion is reality, and ignore what their home looks like, what their finances look like, or what their heart looks like.

When Peter tells us we have all the things we need for life and godliness, he is not telling us to pretend that the rest of your life doesn't count. In fact, what encourages us to grow is the disparity between who we are in Christ and who we are in our daily lives. This gap is the Christian life. This is precisely why we have been given grace and power! If God made our lives instantly perfect, we wouldn't need grace. We have been given all things in order to fill the gap between "sinner" and "saint."

We are never told to pretend the flesh doesn't exist; we are told to stand against it. We do this, however, not from the perspective of the flesh or through religion—following rules to attempt to control the flesh—but from the perspective of God and through His power. We do not pretend to experience something when we don't—this is just craziness. Instead, we pray we will subjectively experience what we know is objectively true.

The second religious trick of the flesh is to get us hyper-focused on the gap, and get us to start thinking that we have to live up to what we have been given—that we have to work to bridge the gap. If we see the first part of life in the Spirit, which is God's perspective of who we are, and see that our life doesn't match up, the temptation is to then try to work harder to get to where we know we should be. This goes back to Paul's question to the Galatians, "Have you begun in the spirit to finish in the flesh?" Unfortunately, it seems that many churches teach this as discipleship. However, this is not discipleship, this is destruction!

It is quite easy to fall into this error. When we see we are supposed to have been set free from lust, anger or envy, it's only natural to think that we have to struggle to subdue these sins, although as Paul explains in Romans, this only makes us want to sin more:

> I know that nothing good lives in me, that is, in my sinful nature. For I have the desire to do what is good, but I cannot carry it out. For what I do is not the good I want to do; no, the evil I do not want to do—this I keep on doing. (Rom. 7:18,19)

If we try to live up to who we are in Christ by our own power, we become worse off emotionally than the person who still lives in the flesh. We have raised the bar, but without any power to reach it. Studies have shown that the least happy people in our culture are conservative, evangelical Christians, because they hold to a high standard to which they believe God has called them, but they are stuck without the power to reach that standard.

If the flesh cannot talk us out of God's perspective, then the flesh will try whatever it can to keep us from God's power. Galatians 5:22-23a says, "But the fruit of the Spirit is love, joy, peace, patience, kindness, goodness, faithfulness, gentleness and self-control." Not the fruit of the law. Not the fruit of self-effort. Not the fruit of trying harder. Not the fruit of discipline. These are the fruit of the Spirit—the things that only the Spirit can produce in us.

Certainly we should obey God's Word, act according to truth, and participate with the Spirit; however, we have to know that *we* don't produce the fruit of the Spirit and *we* don't produce the power to change in the ways we know we should change. It is the fruit of God's Spirit; it's not the fruit of your spirit, or the fruit of any other spirit, but it is purely the fruit of the one and only Holy Spirit present in your life which produces this kind of change. Good old evangelical preaching which is full of God's perspective but without God's power is one-half Spirit and one-half flesh—having a form of godliness but denying its power—and it results in the unhappiest people in this society.

After we get God's perspective, how do we get God's power? The answer is really tough—we simply ask for it. We don't have to subdue our flesh and we don't have to groan and wail and beat ourselves up, at least not if we can rely on the Bible. We obtain God's power by asking for it. Over the years I have noticed over and over how the most disciplined, the most "righteous" people in the church are the least apt to participate in God's power. This is not because they aren't good people or because they are even less deserving than the rest of us; it's simply because they rely on their own power instead of relying on God. God gives power to people because they recognize that they need power and ask for it; and the people who tend to ask are those people who know they aren't going to get it any other way. If you don't think you need God's power, you won't ask for it.

Jesus told us to ask. You have God's perspective, and you know you need God's power. We just have to ask God, who knows how to give good gifts to His children.

The internal conflict is real; it's crazy to deny it, and useless to try to resolve it by human effort. God's perspective says, "Here's where you are, and there's where you're going. Don't fret about the gap; just check back occasionally to see how far you've gone." Again, the gap is why we need grace.

CHAPTER 15: THE RECIPROCAL NATURE OF THE CHURCH

You have probably heard the line, "The church would be really great if it weren't for all the people." This is funny because we all know that the church *is* the people. Furthermore, more than merely an accounting of people who have been "saved," the Church is more properly described as the people of God *in relationship*. We were not set free to live as hermits, spending our lives in quiet contemplation of God. Rather, the Gospel is inherently relational; we were saved into a relationship with God and also with each other as adopted brothers and sisters.

It is understandable, then, that so much of what Paul discusses in his letters concerns this relational aspect of the church. In this regard, Galatians is no different. As Paul shifts from the doctrinal to the practical, the focus is on what the Gospel means in our church relationships.

Paul concludes Chapter 5 with this thought:

> But the fruit of the Spirit is love, joy, peace, patience, kindness, goodness, faithfulness, gentleness and self-control. Against such things there is no law. Those who belong to Christ Jesus have crucified the sinful nature

> with its passions and desires. Since we live by the Spirit, let us keep in step with the Spirit. Let us not become conceited, provoking and envying each other. (Gal. 5:22-26)

Of course, we know Paul had no such chapter division in mind when he was writing. Continuing into Chapter 6, he writes:

> Brothers, if someone is caught in a sin, you who are spiritual should restore him gently. But watch yourself, or you also may be tempted. Carry each other's burdens, and in this way you will fulfill the law of Christ. If anyone thinks he is something when he is nothing, he deceives himself. Each one should test his own actions. Then he can take pride in himself, without comparing himself to somebody else, for each one should carry his own load. (Gal. 6:1-5)

Paul's letter has followed a logical progression, first identifying the problem of legalism sweeping into the Galatian church and nailing down the Gospel issues of salvation and justification. He then explains, as John Wimber used to put it, "The way in is the way on." In other words, we have been saved by grace, not by the Law, and we should therefore live out our Christian lives by grace, not by the Law. Grace never lets us off the hook; rather, grace always *keeps* us off the "hook" of the Law. We are free, to live in grace. Because we are designed to live in community, our relationships should also be built on a foundation of grace, and it is to this that Paul now turns.

The Reciprocal Relationships of the Church

In many churches, the relationships are structured from the top down, in the familiar pyramid-shaped structure we have all seen: The pastors are at the top (under Christ, of course!), followed by a tier of elders and leaders. The pastors and leaders make most of the big decisions and pass them down to the congregation. Those at the top of the pyramid are recognized as the decision-makers (sometimes with "absolute" authority, not requiring approval by the board or the congregation) and they are also the major care-givers for the sheep. When there is a problem, people look to the pastoral staff for help. This is a natural response, as worship services and other church functions are typically focused on the Pastor and the leadership; there is a presumption that those up front must know more than those in the pews. In many churches, this pastor-centered care-giving is intentional, with churches offering a full-time pastoral counseling operation.

Even though it is not specifically taught this way, in many churches with this kind of structure there are often two classes of Christians created, the *Leaders*, and the *Led*. The Leaders are the A-list Christians, the Number Ones. The congregation is second-tier; the Number Two Christians. Paul, however, makes it clear in Galatians and elsewhere, such as 1 Corinthians 12:13-14, that the body of Christ is not a top-down organization; it is reciprocal in nature.

By reciprocal, I mean everyone gives and receives according to their gifts. There is no priestly class, no "Number One's" and "Number Two's;" Christ is the head, our Number One, and we, the body, are all Number Two's, including the head pastor. Some of us have leadership roles and responsibilities, and some are professional (paid) Christians, but we are no further up the spiritual ladder because of our positions. Everybody is expected to give according to their gifts, and receive according to their needs. In 1 Cor. 12:12-13, Paul explains,

> The body is a unit, though it is made up of many parts; and though all its parts are many, they form one body. So it is with Christ. For we were all baptized by one Spirit into one body—whether Jews or Greeks, slave or free—and we were all given the one Spirit to drink.

The Christianity Paul describes is inherently relational. We are part of a body; there is no such thing as "Lone Ranger" Christianity. Paul's use of the human body to describe the Church is important for two reasons. One, we see it is Christ, not the pastor, priest, prophet or pope, who is the head of the Church. The rest of us have different functions, and we all rely on the Head, Jesus. The second reason is, unlike some plants that can be snipped off and grown separately, once you cut a off body part, it's dead. An arm simply cannot survive on its own. Even now when body transplants are done, a thumb, eye or heart is of no use if not connected to a body.

In Galatians 6, Paul tells the Galatians essentially the same thing: We are all to carry the burdens of others, and he implies in this statement that we are also to allow others to carry our burdens. This does not describe a top-down or pyramid-shaped organization, this describes the church as "flat"—a collection of reciprocal relationships. Paul does not mention anything about relying on the pastors or leaders to guide you or direct you; he does not say, "If you have a burden, call the church office." What Paul does say is quite different from this, carrying a number of important assumptions and implications.

First, Paul assumes the church was connected relationally, and the members of the Galatian church knew each other well enough that people would either know each other's burdens, or would volunteer this information. This is quite different than the "don't ask, don't tell" atmosphere we see in many of our churches, where silence is not only golden, it's expected.

Many churches today have a different problem, which is simply their size. If you are in a church of one or two hundred people, chances are the majority will know who you are, and chances are you have invited each other over for dinner. However, if you are in a church of several hundred—or several thousand—it is easy to slip in and out on a Sunday morning without anyone knowing you were even there. This problem is fairly easy to overcome, but it needs commitment on the part of the church as well as the individual members: It requires that the church provide some type of relational small groups where people can easily connect with each other, and it also requires people to make the effort to connect in one or more of these groups. A third approach is simply for people reach out to those sitting around them, to make sure everyone has an opportunity to connect. We are all equals in this endeavor; we all have the obligation to reach out in relationship to those around us, whether we are one of the founding members or a newcomer.

We All Have Our Burdens

Notice the underlying assumption in Galatians 6:2: We all have burdens. In general, people in the church have been trained to deny or suppress their problems and pain in order to be accepted. This is true of many "holiness" and fundamentalist churches but is also, I think, true in general of the American church—especially if you come from a rather stoic heritage, where pain and suffering is considered a way of life. We are rugged individualists, self-reliant and proud; we don't need anyone or anything, especially if it appears to be a hand-out. If someone helps us out, we put ourselves under obligation to pay them back. We have already talked about how this is totally contrary to grace and the Gospel—as soon as we start trying to pay for something, it ceases to be a gift.

However, this attitude is often taught by the church! Churches, like any secular corporation, are quite Darwinian in nature; that is, it functions on a "survival of the fittest" mentality. If you can suck it up long enough, if you can manage your sin well enough, if you can keep from being exposed long enough, you will be seen as an elder and asked to move up to a higher position. However, should you dare to suggest you have a problem, especially something on the current top-ten sin list, you're toast. You might as well go find a new church, because you will be branded a sinner forever, or at the very least, a spiritual loser.

Sometimes this attitude starts with the smiling pastor who always has easy answers and glib advice for problems. The only times he mentions his own struggles are in the past tense, to tell you how he was victorious. He gives us lists of things to do to ensure we live a nice, safe, sin-managed life. And, perhaps we are told another lie, that if we do the Christian thing properly, we won't have any problems, and our lives will be successful. But if we have struggles, we show we haven't been doing the Christian "thing" right, so therefore we must be in sin—in this dynamic, confessing sin produces shame. And what happens when we are ashamed? We hide.

What is being modeled for us by these "holy" pastors is the idea that what you look like is more important than what you are. Many years ago I [Alden] found a humorous get-well card to send to my brother-in-law. On the front it said, "It's not how you feel, it's how you look." Then on the inside was the line, "after all, no one really cares how you feel." While I still think the card was hilarious (and luckily so does he), what is sad is that this is all too often really true.

Don't Always Blame The Pastor

You can see what these teachings do to both our ability to function in grace, and the ability to follow Paul's advice in his letter to the Galatians—it prevents it completely! Now here's something which may surprise you: Lest you think pastors are always the bad guys, often the pressure to look holy is even greater for them! The problems of the pyramid-shaped church go both ways; not only is there pressure exerted from the top down, there is also pressure exerted from the bottom up. The pastor is always expected to be the most holy, the most knowledgeable, and the most perfect role model in the church. Rather than seeing the pastor as an equal with a different function, he's put on the proverbial pedestal, and often with god-like expectations. It's not fair, and it isn't Biblical. How could a pastor withstand these kinds of expectations without failing? Even if he never expresses it, he knows in his heart he doesn't live up to the congregations' expectations. So, what else can a pastor do but keep up the image, and in turn push these expectations back down to the congregation? It really is a self-perpetuating cycle.

I [Alden] know of a former associate pastor who was assigned the task of teaching a small group Bible study. He threw himself into it, and worked hard at building relationships. However, he made a fatal mistake, daring to share some of his own struggles with the group and asking them to pray for him. The rest of the leadership—all wonderful, well-meaning people—found out about this "error," and the young pastor was severely chastised for his "indiscretion." He was told as a leader he should never share his struggles with those in the church, as he had a responsibility to maintain his good role-model image. This is not an unusual story, by any means, but it illustrates two errors common to many churches: The church leadership failed first of all to recognize the equality which exists in the church, and secondly failed to recognize the reciprocal nature of church relationships which Paul so clearly taught.

Paul, however, expects us to have burdens, whether we are new Christians or the senior pastor. The question is not whether or not we will have burdens, but rather, will we share them with others and will we help carry the burdens of others. Your burdens are real and tangible to you, and you are to make your burdens real and tangible to others. Give others in the church "handles" to grab hold of your burdens, so they can help carry them. Don't suppress and hide your burdens, or even downplay them with comments like, "I don't want to weigh you down with all the details, please just pray for me, however you feel led." This sounds spiritual, but it is pure malarkey. When you down-play your struggles, you are playing Lone Ranger, or a James Dean-like "rebel without a clue." One thing you are *not* doing is acting like a member of the Church.

Another Problem with the Pyramid-Shaped Church

If a church is designed so that the Pastors and leaders do all of the burden-carrying, we have another problem: It is completely impossible for a handful of leaders to carry the burdens of even a small church; however, this is what pastors are taught and expected to do. I [Ken] was a physical and emotional wreck as a pastor before I discovered this truth; I had ulcers, chronic back pain, and I was half nuts trying to be the ideal pastor. It was by sheer necessity that I finally looked in the Bible for some answers, and what I found was it was not the job of the pastors to carry the burdens for the church; the ministry was the people's job all along! The pastor's job is not to carry the whole load; it is to train the people to carry the burden of the ministry.

Of course, to make this work, it becomes obvious that "church" can't merely be focused on Sunday mornings. This is why I have been such a proponent of small groups, where people can relate to each other and actually share each other's burdens through prayer as well as practical assistance if called for. Ministry, as defined by Paul, is a grassroots effort of reciprocal relationships. In business terms, it is a "flat" organization, with the primary relationships being horizontal rather than being vertically connected to the Pastor. I believe this so much that in the last church that I pastored, we had no formal membership; it was completely relational and based on small group involvement. If you belonged to a home group, you were a part of the church. It was as simple as that. My primary function as pastor was to teach and be a resource to others.

Share Burdens, but Carry Loads

Paul writes in verse 5, "... each should carry his own load." Now on the surface this may seem to be a contradiction with sharing burdens, but this is a case where knowing a little Greek helps. The Greek words for "burden" and "load" are entirely different words. "Burden," the word used in verse 2, means, "heavy, crushing, and awkward to carry." The word used in verse 5 for "load" is a word that essentially means "backpack." It is the word used for the pack carried by soldiers. Those of you that have loads which are difficult or impossible to carry alone, ask for help. I am reminded of the warnings on the boxes of assemble-at-home furniture that say "two man load." It's actually stupid to try to manage one of those things by yourself.

On the other hand, be responsible for the cares of everyday life, like paying your bills, raising your children, cleaning your house, reading your Bible, and so on. If you have a job to do, do it well. Be responsible. Paul wants us to have the dignity of behaving like mature adults, or at least growing into mature adults. I've known people who have taken the concept of sharing burdens to the extreme; they run to everyone for every little problem, often looking for prophetic words for common sense tasks like what kind of bread to buy. Paul recognizes that in doing so, we lose all self-respect (besides becoming totally wacky), so he encourages the Galatians individually to honestly assess what they are capable of. We should have enough pride to "carry our own weight," but not so much pride that we deny our need in situations in which we require assistance. In practical terms, if you have a financial emergency, ask for help; however, don't expect a weekly support check from the church while you sit on the couch and watch Oprah, as long as you are able to work. As Paul said elsewhere, if you don't work, you don't eat. If you don't have a job, volunteer.

Note that Paul started off this discussion with an example of burden-carrying:

> Brothers, if someone is caught in a sin, you who are spiritual should restore him gently. But watch yourself, or you also may be tempted. (Gal. 6:1)

A person caught in a sin is definitely carrying a burden and in need of help, and we are to do something about it: We are to intervene, in an attempt to correct and restore this person.

When we see someone fall into sin, we shouldn't ignore it, gossip about it, or take the false position that we are either too forgiving or too mature to let someone else's sin become an issue for us. This is to totally miss the point; this is not what our perspective should be about sin. The point is that the other person is in trouble and is in need of help. In compassion and love, we are supposed to help to carry their burden by restoring them to wholeness.

The purpose of confronting sin is not to judge or assign blame. Remember Jesus' words,

> Be merciful, just as your Father is merciful. "Do not judge, and you will not be judged. Do not condemn, and you will not be condemned. Forgive, and you will be forgiven. (Luke 6:36,37)

If you read carefully through the Gospel accounts, you will see where Jesus often hinted at a different view of sin than many of us have been taught—Jesus saw sin as a curse, a plague upon mankind, a sickness—something to be healed. Consider his comments at the healing of the paralytic in Matthew 9:5,6:

> Which is easier: to say, 'Your sins are forgiven,' or to say, 'Get up and walk'? But so that you may know that the Son of Man has authority on earth to forgive sins...." Then he said to the paralytic, "Get up, take your mat and go home."

What a strange comparison to make, unless sin has qualities in common with sickness and requires healing. When we approach someone burdened by sin, it should be with this kind of an attitude, not condemnation. Otherwise, rather than lifting burdens, we add to the person's burden by loading them down with guilt and condemnation.

Take another look at the first verse in Galatians 6, and see to whom Paul is writing: "... you who are spiritual should restore him gently." From what Paul has written, I think we can draw a couple of conclusions. First, he is not writing to the church leadership, he is directing this whole letter to the entire church in Galatia. He makes no attempt at pulling the leaders aside for some pastoral training; he is clearly addressing these comments to the Galatians at large. Confronting sin and restoring those afflicted by sin, therefore, is not an exclusive job of the pastor or leaders. No, this job falls on those in the church, those "who are spiritual."

Who Is Spiritual?

This now begs the obvious question, "Who are the spiritual ones in the church?" Consider again who Paul is writing to—these are the Galatians, the people Paul has just accused of being foolish and bewitched. Paul is simply continuing his thought about the proper Christian life. Spiritual people are those who are operating from God's perspective and under God's power, a life under grace, not legalism. One again, if you are operating from God's perspective, you are "in the Spirit"—you are a spiritual person. In other words, Paul is talking to Christians. It is the job of everyone who believes the Gospel to come to the rescue of those burdened by sin.

Operating in God's perspective and in the power of the Spirit means operating in grace, healing, and forgiveness. It is not trying to restore someone with either sentimentality or judgmentalism. It is not using pop psychology, trendy counseling methods, self-help books, or advice from your own experience and perspective. Operating in the Spirit means restoring people from the perspective of God's Word, under the direction and power of the Holy Spirit.

I have heard it said that the church is the only army that kills its own wounded. Many Christians could use some lessons in basic manners, alongside some theology. Perhaps this is what Paul had in mind when he issued the warning, "But watch yourself, or you also may be tempted." If we do not approach an issue of sin in complete humility and submission to Christ, then we set ourselves up for sin as well, whether pride, arrogance, judgmentalism, or any number of other sins. We would do well to remember John Bradford's famous line, "There but for the grace of God, go I."

Think of it this way: We can't help carry someone's burden unless we put ourselves on equal terms with that person. If we can't do this, then at the very least we should keep our mouths shut. But we should also follow the rest of Paul's advice and test our actions; perhaps we have our own sin burden for which we need to seek help.

Paul's final comment in this section dealing with the reciprocal nature of church relationships concerns the teacher-student relationship, "Anyone who receives instruction in the word must share all good things with his instructor." The implication here is once again fairly obvious: The student has received good things from the instructor, but there are no one-way relationships in the church. We, too, are to share our gifts. Church is not meant to be a one-way street, a unilateral download of teaching and information from the pastor. No, he who teaches you should also expect to receive from you "all good things."

Now, About Tithing ...

"All good things" is usually interpreted in our culture to mean we should support our teachers financially, and this is perhaps unfortunate that in our culture "all good things" has been reduced to money. (It also raises the question of why Sunday School teachers are never paid, but let's not go there.) Furthermore, teaching on this verse often drifts into a teaching about tithing, and winds right back into legalism, completely ignoring the point of the entire letter to the Galatians.

The interesting thing about the New Testament teaching on money and giving is that it too is relational; the New Testament does not treat giving in a religious or legalistic manner. You can teach tithing as a good financial principle, but you cannot teach tithing as a law under the New Testament without undoing everything Paul has taught about the law and grace. Giving, as taught by Paul, is purely an act of reciprocal love for one another. This puts a whole new spin on the issue of giving, and takes all of the guilt, pressure, superstition, and manipulation out of it. As I discussed earlier, teaching freedom often results in a state of fear for the pastor; I think this is why hardly anyone looks too closely at what the New Testament actually teaches about tithing.

Let me say this one more time very clearly: The common teaching that says you must tithe (ten percent or as much as you can squeeze out of your income) to your local church is not only *not* supportable by the New Testament, it is *contrary* to the New Testament. This teaching is designed to put you under the Law, so that you can be manipulated. You can't buy God off financially, just like you can't buy God off any other way, and you will not be punished or deserted by God for failing to give your full ten percent. Giving, like the rest of the Christian life, is an act of grace and love.

Because God have given us all good things, we *must* also give. The word "must" in this verse does not mean you must give "or else," but rather, we are all compelled by gratitude and the Spirit of Christ to share all good things with one another. Once we have received so freely, it is our natural, Spirit-led response to give—the more like Christ we become, the harder it is for us *not* to give.

If there is one thing that I am hoping you pick up from this book, it is that whether you are dealing with salvation, your quiet time, your relationships, or your money, the New Testament attitude toward it is firmly grounded in grace. The Gospel message is not merely about "getting saved." The Gospel—the Good News—is that *everything* is through grace, and it is for this reason we should be preaching the Good News to each other on a regular basis. As I pointed out earlier, the world tells you lie after lie about who you are and how you should perform. Only a constant diet of grace will allow us to remain and continue to live as free men and women.

CHAPTER 16: WHAT GOES AROUND COMES AROUND, OR YOU REAP WHAT YOU SOW

> When I have Christian righteousness reigning in my heart, I descend from heaven as the rain makes fruitful the earth; that is to say, I do good works, how and wheresoever the occasion arises. If I am a minister of the Word, I preach, I comfort the brokenhearted, I administer the sacraments. If I am a householder, I govern my house and family well, and in the fear of God. If I am a servant, I do my master's business faithfully. —From Martin Luther's introduction to his Commentary on Galatians

It is often thought that teaching the Gospel of radical grace is opposed to doing good works; however, nothing is further from the truth. The question is not whether or not to do good works, but in what context we do them; there is nothing incongruous here. As strong as Paul was in his position that good works had no place in either producing either salvation or holiness, he writes in chapter 6:7-10:

> Do not be deceived: God cannot be mocked. A man reaps what he sows. The one who sows to please his

> sinful nature, from that nature will reap destruction; the one who sows to please the Spirit, from the Spirit will reap eternal life. Let us not become weary in doing good, for at the proper time we will reap a harvest if we do not give up. Therefore, as we have opportunity, let us do good to all people, especially to those who belong to the family of believers.

This passage, especially verse 7, should be familiar to all of you. I would venture to guess this might be the most preached-on verse in Galatians, especially since it can be conveniently excised from the rest of the chapter and slid nicely into a works-oriented, hell-fire and holiness message. So, let us remind ourselves of the context in which Paul wrote this and unwrap it a bit.

Paul wrote this letter to the Galatians specifically to address a legalistic teaching that had crept in to the Galatian church which had the effect of destroying the Gospel message Paul had preached to them. He has spent several pages laying out the basic premise that "the written law kills, but the Spirit gives life," and explaining how both justification and sanctification—salvation and living the Christian life as the Spirit changes us—are solely grace-oriented. He then outlined the horizontal, reciprocal and servant nature of church relationships, showing how grace is at the center of all aspects of the Christian life. Now, he takes an apparent turn—or does he?

"Do not be deceived, God cannot be mocked." Paul has already accused the Galatians of being deceived; in fact, he accused them of being bewitched, because they fell for a false gospel message in which grace was not sufficient to complete the Christian life. The infiltrators, of course, had been pushing the Jewish Law—circumcision, in fact—as necessary to be "real" Christians. Paul now comes at the same issue from a different perspective: the principle of reaping and sowing.

The analogy is, of course, fairly obvious. If you plant apple seeds you'll get apple trees; you have no chance whatsoever of getting oranges, unless you have mixed up your seeds. I [Ken] grew up on a farm, where I learned that a wheat seed and a deadly nightshade seed look quite similar; however, if you plant them, you will find that one will feed you and the other will kill you. What you plant is important. Now, Paul is not talking about "seed-faith" or any mechanistic formulas for success, he is only stating an obvious principle of nature.

Paul's goal for the Galatians was for them to learn to live according to the Spirit, and this, of course, is still relevant to us today. However, if we don't live a life of the Spirit as Paul has described, if this is not where we are putting our faith and energy, then we can't reap spiritual benefits. Sowing bad seeds, whether these seeds are a life of sin or a life of looking to the Law for our holiness and salvation, will lead to destruction. Sowing good seeds, living a life of faith, produces life.

It seems to me that Paul was also speaking rather practically here. We can "mock God" by claiming grace, but at the same time living a mean, nasty, selfish life. In this case we aren't living according to the Spirit; we are serving ourselves, not living by grace, but using grace as an excuse. As Paul asked the Romans, "should we sin more so grace will increase?" The obvious answer, which Paul confirms, is "Absolutely not!" Once again, "It is for freedom that Christ has set us free" (Gal. 5:1). We cannot live a life of sowing sin-seeds and claim freedom; this is *not* why we were set free. One of the fruits of sin is bondage, and therefore incongruent with freedom.

"You reap what you sow" has, of course, obvious implications. If you spend your entire life overeating, you should know why you are obese; don't be surprised, and don't blame your parents for not raising you properly. If you have treated your spouse with disrespect for years, don't be surprised if your marriage fails. The converse rule, which Paul states here, is simple: If you want your marriage to improve, start sowing good seeds. If you want to get in better shape, start exercising, eating healthy and taking vitamins. If you want to understand God better, start praying and reading your Bible. These things are, as they say, "no-brainers."

This is not legalism, this is just common sense! As in the earlier few verses, Paul expects us, as Christians under grace, to act like mature adults, "each carrying our own load." Living a life controlled by the Spirit is not living a slacker lifestyle, counting on God and your friends for handouts. As Paul wrote to the Thessalonians, "If a man will not work, he shall not eat" (2 Thess. 3:10). Living by the Spirit means investing in the things of the Spirit, and of course expecting the Holy Spirit to provide the power and ability to grow and mature.

So, Paul encourages us to "not be weary in doing good," promising we will indeed reap the benefits of our good-deed-doing. What often gets to people is the time-lag inherent in any growing process. You do not plant seeds one day and reap the next; plants take time to grow (unless, it seems, they're weeds). Spiritual seeds we sow in our own lives and the lives of others by loving, caring, serving, worshipping, and reading the Bible do not mature overnight, although you could see some fairly instantaneous fruit. But if the fruit you hope for doesn't appear overnight, don't fret; know that if you sow good seeds, someday you will indeed reap a good harvest.

Doing good works will not earn us any salvation-points or holiness-points; this is not the purpose of good works. We are saved and justified by grace, and we are being made holy—into the very likeness of God—by grace. It is precisely because we are being made into God's likeness that we do good works, because this is what God does—He does good works. This is why we have been set free: So we can be conformed into Christ's image, thinking, feeling, and acting like God, more and more each day. Works are not a requirement; they are our destiny.

Back to Circumcision

Finally, to finish this thought and bring it back full circle, Paul concludes with:

> Those who want to make a good impression outwardly are trying to compel you to be circumcised. The only reason they do this is to avoid being persecuted for the cross of Christ. Not even those who are circumcised obey the law, yet they want you to be circumcised that they may boast about your flesh. May I never boast except in the cross of our Lord Jesus Christ, through which the world has been crucified to me, and I to the world. Neither circumcision nor uncircumcision means anything; what counts is a new creation. Peace and mercy to all who follow this rule, even to the Israel of God. (Gal. 6:12-16)

Those who were sowing legalistic seeds and not living according to the Spirit were trying to convince the Galatians to become Jews under the Law, not according to the Spirit. Again, Paul emphasizes the distinction between the Law and the Gospel, saying, "neither circumcision nor uncircumcision mean anything; what counts is a new creation." The goal of the Christian life is not to look good, nor is it to please the rules of men. It is not even to feel good about yourself or to do good to others (if you are only doing good to earn spiritual points).

What matters is that in Christ, by *sola gratia*—grace alone—you have been made a new creation, so you can live life not as a prisoner under the law, but as a free man or woman who is being changed from glory to glory into the image of God. It is indeed for freedom that Christ has set us free.

CHAPTER 17: BACK TO THE BEGINNING

It seems fitting that we should also come full circle and close where we began, at the reason Paul's Letter to the Galatians is crucial for us today. Once again, here is how Martin Luther begins his Introduction to his 2nd Commentary on the Epistle to the Galatians:

> I have taken in hand, in the name of the Lord, once again to expound the Epistle of St. Paul to the Galatians; not because I desire to teach new things, or such as you have not heard before, but because we have to fear, as the greatest and nearest danger, that Satan take from us the pure doctrine of faith and bring into the Church again the doctrine of works and men's traditions.
>
> The devil, our adversary, who continually seeks to devour us, is not dead; likewise our flesh and old man is yet alive. Besides this, all kinds of temptations vex and oppress us on every side. So this doctrine can never be taught, urged, and repeated enough. If this doctrine is lost, then is also the whole knowledge of the truth, life and salvation lost. If this doctrine flourishes, then all good things flourish.

Luther had seen and experienced what happens when the Church loses the Gospel, turning instead to a religion based on works. Not only had he fought the errors of the medieval Roman Catholic Church, but he had also witnessed the rise of various Anabaptist groups who he saw also substituted a false gospel based on works rather than the true Gospel as taught by Paul. The Anabaptists, among other things, were teaching that pacifism, separation from the world, and refusing to own private property made them more holy than other Christians. Luther recognized that "the greatest and nearest danger" to the Church was the loss of the pure Gospel message, writing, "...this doctrine can never be taught, urged, and repeated enough."

It is for this same reason that I continue to preach the Gospel of radical grace. Unfortunately, many people fail to see legalism as a threat. Instead, they mistakenly let things slide under the erroneous guise of grace! Those standing against legalism are often written off as being overly critical and judgmental. Grace, it seems, has become confused with tolerance. But as G.K. Chesterton said, "Tolerance is the virtue of a man with no convictions." I am admittedly intolerant of legalism. I am also often quite angry that people are misled, abused, and robbed of the Gospel. I believe this is of utmost importance—to quote Luther once again, "If this doctrine is lost, then is also the whole knowledge of the truth, life and salvation lost."

It is my desire that in these pages you have found truth, and by this truth been set free. I also hope the words of Paul have convinced you of the crucial importance of knowing the pure Gospel, and hope that this message has also become yours.

For it is for freedom that Christ has set us free.

Alden Swan

THANKS

Many thanks to my son, Isaiah, for doing an incredible editing job, and to Julia Loren for her final editing and making me change the title of the book (again!). Thanks to my family—Jo, Elliot, Isaiah, and Elizabeth—for living with me through this process. Thanks to the Evans for the use of their beach house to finish the first draft. Finally, thanks to Ken for his friendship, inspiration and encouragement, and for preaching such a great sermon series.

Alden

LaVergne, TN USA
01 November 2010
203058LV00001B/1/P